THE COMPLETE AIR FRYER COOKBOOK

THE COMPLETE AIR FRYER COOKBOOK

Over 100 easy, energy-efficient recipes for every meal

CONTENTS

SUPER EASY GUIDE TO AIR FRYERS

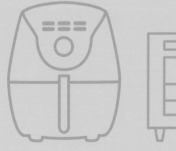

HOW THEY WORK

The air fryer is renowned for replicating the crisp texture of deep-fried foods using a fraction of the oil. This amped-up countertop convection oven works by pushing hot air around food; the rapid circulation of air in the confined space helps make food crisp, just like deep-frying but with much less oil. For example, air-fried french fries contain just 4–6g fat versus 17g for deep-fried ones.

THE DIFFERENT TYPES OF AIR FRYERS

There are many different sizes and shapes of air fryers available, from compact spaceship-looking styles, which sit upright and have a deep pull-out drawer, to air fryers that look like mini ovens. These are also designed to sit on a counter, but they are less compact and more comparable in size to a microwave oven.

BASKET AIR FRYERS These compact versions range in capacity from 3–4 quarts to 6–7 quarts and are typically the more affordable option. With this style, the base of the handled basket is perforated and slightly elevated above the bottom of the pan, which collects oil drippings and cooking juices. While they are nifty, they do not allow for large volumes of food, and you will not be able to cook an entire family meal in them.

OVEN AIR FRYERS These larger versions of air fryers (11 quarts) open like an oven with a door. They offer the convenience of a compact oven with the benefits of an air fryer and, for a single person or couple, could even suffice as your only cooking medium. These appliances come equipped with two or three wire racks for shelves, which allow for a variety of foods being cooked at the same time. They also include additional functions, such as a low-temperature mode for dehydrating and a defrost mode for thawing food. As well, they come with preset functions for cooking foods such as chips and fries, chops, shrimp, chicken drumsticks, and steaks. The clear oven door allows you to see how the cooking is progressing without the need to open it, keeping the temperature stable inside. Naturally, with these additional benefits, the price tag for these larger appliances is higher, ranging from the low hundreds and upward.

For this book, we've used popular well-priced and midsize 5.3-quart and 7-quart models. We have also used the dehydrator function of a larger 11-quart three-in-one air fryer. If you have a larger appliance, you will be able to cook larger amounts of food, while for a smaller one, you will need to decrease quantities accordingly to fit in your appliance.

SAFETY

Before using your air fryer, carefully read the manufacturer's instructions for your appliance.

Air fryers can get hot, so allow sufficient space on the countertop around it. The vent at the back extracts steam and, with it, grease, so you will find that you need to wipe down the surface behind your air fryer.

Once the basket is pulled out of the appliance, treat it as if it has come out of the oven—it will be hot! Take care when adding and removing items from the air-fryer basket.

It is also important to clean your appliance after every use, both the inner basket and the outer pan, to remove grease; otherwise, the appliance will smoke and any small trapped pieces of food will burn.

FRYING

Air fryers excel at crisping dry ingredients, but where they don't work well is for foods with wet batters—the batter will simply stick rather than get crispy. It is also not just a case of popping food into the air fryer instead of into hot oil in a pan. The cooking method needs to be adapted to create a comparable result.

THE OTHER STUFF

The air fryer is far more than a single-use appliance for making crunchy, crispy fries. For starters, it helps to think past the name, which is a bit of a misnomer. The appliance is not a deep fryer at all and actually offers many of the benefits an oven does.

Its major limitation is the interior capacity; be sure that the dish or dishes you plan to use in your air fryer are heatproof and will fit in the appliance with room for air to circulate. Avoid any that are too tall and will come in contact with the top element of the appliance; otherwise, the food will burn.

If you are using the appliance to bake, avoid very light-textured or liquidy batters, as the vortex created by the appliance is strong enough to make the batter spit or create a volcanic-looking top on your baked item.

Keep an eye on sugary mixtures, since in an air fryer, browning will be accelerated.

For success, you will want to have an oil sprayer or mister. Some recipes call for an oil spray on foods. Avoid aerosol cooking sprays as they will damage your air fryer's basket.

5 BEST FOODS TO COOK IN THE AIR FRYER

ACCESSORIES

Racks Most basket-style air fryers come equipped with at least one basic circular rack. Also useful is a toast rack to assist with bread slices sitting upright.

Pans Investing in cake pans that fit in your appliance will enable you to get the most out of it. Many small conventional pans will fit. Muffin pans for standard ovens won't, so buy a circular tray with muffin inserts.

Utensils While most everyday kitchen utensils such as tongs and spatulas can be used in the air fryer, it is worth investing in ones with silicone ends, if you want to maintain the protective surface of your appliance.

Small silicone mats Small silicone mats are perfect for lining the bottom of the air fryer when cooking baked goods, as parchment paper will fly up. You can find these inexpensive mats at budget and homeware stores, and cut to size to fit your appliance.

1 **ROAST VEGGIES**

2 **CRISP CHICKPEAS**

3 **BREADED FOODS**

4 **PIZZA & CALZONES**

5 **MEATBALLS & SAUSAGES**

HEALTHIER SNACKS

Convenience and satisfaction are key when it comes to snacks. With the air fryer, you can create healthy, tempting snacks instead of reaching for junk food filled with empty calories or laden with sugar.

CAULIFLOWER PHYLLO TRIANGLES

1 small onion, cut into
   thin wedges
1lb (225g) cauliflower,
   finely chopped
2 garlic cloves, crushed
½ tsp ground turmeric
½ tsp ground ginger
¼ tsp ground cinnamon,
   plus extra, to dust
extra-virgin olive oil for misting
2½oz (75g) feta, crumbled
2 tbsp roasted chopped almonds
2 tbsp coarsely chopped cilantro
2 tbsp coarsely chopped
   flat-leaf parsley
12 sheets of phyllo pastry
to serve: lemon wedges and cilantro
   leaves

1 Preheat a 5.3-quart air fryer to 350°F/180°C for 3 minutes.
2 Combine onion, cauliflower, and garlic in a medium bowl, then sprinkle with combined spices; spray generously with olive oil.
3 Carefully line the air-fryer basket with parchment paper. Put the cauliflower mixture in the basket; cook for 5 minutes, until cauliflower is tender.
4 Transfer cooked cauliflower mixture to a bowl. Add feta, almonds, and herbs to the bowl; stir to combine. Let cool. (Alternatively, spread out mixture on a sheet pan and place in the freezer to chill for 5 minutes.)
5 Stack 2 sheets of pastry together, spraying between layers with olive oil. Cut stacked pastry lengthwise into three strips. Place a heaped tablespoon of cauliflower mixture in the corner of one pastry strip, leaving a ½in (1cm) border. Fold opposite corner of pastry diagonally across filling to form a triangle; continue folding to the end of the pastry strip, retaining the triangular shape. Place, seam-side down, on a sheet pan. Repeat with remaining pastry sheets and cauliflower mixture to make a total of 18 phyllo triangles. Spray triangles with olive oil; dust with extra cinnamon.
6 Place half of the phyllo triangles in the basket; cook for 10 minutes. Turn triangles over; cook for a further 10 minutes, until golden. Transfer to a wire rack. Repeat cooking with remaining phyllo triangles.
7 Serve phyllo triangles with lemon wedges and cilantro leaves.

**prep + cook time 1 hour (+ cooling)
makes 18**

GREEN FALAFEL
& TAHINI SAUCE

2½ cups (375g) frozen edamame
  beans
1 x 15oz (425g) can chickpeas,
  drained and rinsed
1 medium onion, chopped
3 garlic cloves
1 cup (30g) coarsely chopped
  flat-leaf parsley
½ cup (25g) coarsely chopped mint
1 cup (50g) coarsely chopped
  cilantro
½ cup (75g) all-purpose flour
1 tsp fine salt
2 tsp ground cumin
1 tsp Moroccan spice mix
extra-virgin olive oil for misting
to serve: chargrilled pita bread,
  extra herbs, and lemon wedges

TAHINI SAUCE
½ cup (140g) Greek-style yogurt
1½ tbsp tahini
1 garlic clove, crushed
2 tsp lemon juice
salt and pepper to taste

1 Place frozen edamame beans in a bowl; pour over boiling water. Let stand for 1 minute; drain. Cool under cold running water. Blend or process 2 cups (300g) of the edamame beans, the chickpeas, onion, garlic, herbs, flour, salt, cumin, and spice mix until finely chopped. Shape heaped tablespoons of mixture into approximately 26 oval falafel; place on a sheet pan lined with parchment paper. Refrigerate for 1 hour to firm.
2 Meanwhile, to make tahini sauce, whisk ingredients in a small bowl until smooth; season to taste.
3 Preheat a 5.3-quart air fryer to 350°F/180°C for 3 minutes.
4 Spray falafel generously with olive oil. Carefully place half of the falafel in the air-fryer basket; cook for 12 minutes, turning halfway through cooking time, or until golden. Transfer to a plate; cover to keep warm. Repeat cooking with the remaining falafel.
5 Fill chargrilled pita bread with falafel, remaining edamame, and extra herbs; drizzle with tahini sauce. Serve with lemon wedges.

TIP Sprinkle the tahini sauce with Moroccan spice mix, if you like.

**prep + cook time
40 minutes
(+ refrigeration)
serves 4**

SUN-DRIED TOMATO & FETA POLENTA FRIES

3 cups (750ml) chicken or
   vegetable stock
1 cup (170g) instant polenta
2 tbsp (30g) butter, chopped
½ cup (40g) finely grated Parmesan
   cheese
3oz (90g) sun-dried tomatoes,
   no added oil, finely chopped
⅓ cup (20g) chopped basil leaves
3½oz (100g) feta, crumbled
olive oil for misting
to serve: sea salt flakes

SALSA VERDE
2 tbsp red wine vinegar
2 tbsp capers, coarsely chopped
1 shallot, finely chopped
½ cup (25g) basil leaves,
   coarsely chopped
1 cup (20g) flat-leaf parsley leaves,
   coarsely chopped
½ cup (125ml) extra-virgin olive oil

1 Bring stock to a boil in a large, deep saucepan; add polenta in a thin, steady stream, whisking until the mixture comes to a boil. Reduce heat to low; cook, stirring with a long-handled wooden spoon or whisk, for 10 minutes, until mixture is soft and thick. Stir in butter, Parmesan cheese, sun-dried tomatoes, and basil.

2 Grease a deep 8in (20cm) square cake pan; line bottom and sides with parchment paper. Spread half of the polenta mixture over the bottom of the pan; sprinkle with half of the feta. Spread remaining polenta over feta; sprinkle with remaining feta, pressing it gently into the polenta. Cover pan. Refrigerate for 3 hours.

3 Preheat a 7-quart air fryer to 400°F/200°C for 3 minutes.

4 Turn out polenta onto a cutting board and cut into 18 pieces; spray generously all over with oil.

5 Spray the air-fryer basket with oil. Carefully place polenta fries in the basket; cook for 15 minutes, turning halfway through cooking time, or until golden brown and crisp.

6 Meanwhile, to make salsa verde, combine ingredients in a bowl.

7 Sprinkle polenta fries with sea salt flakes and serve with salsa verde.

**prep + cook time
50 minutes
(+ refrigeration)
makes 18**

TIP Smooth ricotta is available in tubs in the refrigerated section of the supermarket.

HERB BAKED RICOTTA
WITH VEGGIE DIPPERS

2 x 2oz (60g) round flatbreads
1 tbsp (10g) butter, melted
½ tsp Italian-style dried herb mix
16oz (500g) thick smooth ricotta
   (see tip)
1 egg, lightly beaten
⅓ cup (25g) finely grated Parmesan
   cheese
1 tbsp thyme leaves
¼ tsp dried chili flakes
salt and pepper to taste
to serve: extra thyme leaves,
   extra-virgin olive oil, baby rainbow
   carrots, baby cucumbers,
   radishes, and Little Gem lettuce

1 Preheat a 7-quart air fryer to 350°F/180°C for 3 minutes.
2 Brush flatbread rounds with butter and sprinkle herb mix over the top.
3 Carefully place one of the flatbread rounds in the air-fryer basket, then place a wire rack on top; cook for 3 minutes or until golden and crisp. Transfer to a plate to cool. Repeat cooking with remaining flatbread round. Once cooled, cut flatbread rounds into wedges.
4 Meanwhile, place ricotta, egg, Parmesan cheese, thyme, and chili flakes in a medium bowl, then season with salt and pepper; stir to combine. Divide mixture between two 10oz (300ml) ovenproof baking dishes.
5 Place dishes in the air-fryer basket; cook for 20 minutes, until ricotta is golden and set. Remove dishes from the air fryer.
6 Sprinkle baked ricottas with extra thyme leaves and drizzle with olive oil. Serve warm with flatbread wedges, baby carrots, baby cucumbers, radishes, and lettuce.

**prep + cook time
40 minutes serves 6**

TIP You can find spring roll wrappers in the freezer section of Asian grocers and supermarkets. Thaw before using.

VEGETABLE SPRING ROLLS

1½oz (50g) dried vermicelli
   rice noodles
1 garlic clove, crushed
2 tbsp finely chopped fresh ginger
1 shallot, thinly sliced
1 large carrot, cut into matchsticks
2 cups (160g) shredded napa
   cabbage
½ tsp Chinese five-spice powder
1 tsp sesame oil
2 tsp peanut oil
2 tbsp tamari
1 tsp cornstarch
10 x 8¾in (21.5cm) frozen spring roll
   wrappers, thawed (see tip)
oil for misting
to serve: cilantro leaves
   and lime wedges

1 Place vermicelli in a medium bowl of boiling water for 2 minutes until soft; drain well. Using scissors, snip noodles into shorter lengths.

2 Line the basket of a 5.3-quart air fryer with parchment paper, then place garlic, ginger, shallot, carrot, cabbage, five-spice powder, and sesame and peanut oils in the basket; toss to combine. Set temperature to 350°F/180°C; cook for 5 minutes, until vegetables are soft.

3 Carefully transfer vegetable mixture to a bowl. Combine tamari and cornstarch in a separate, small bowl. Add cornstarch mixture to vegetable mixture with vermicelli; toss to combine. Let cool to room temperature.

4 Place a spring roll wrapper on a flat work surface. Place ¼ cup of the filling in a line one-third up from the bottom edge, leaving a ¾in (1.5cm) border on each side. Fold over once, then fold in the sides and roll up to enclose filling; brush the join with a little water to seal. Repeat with remaining spring roll wrappers and filling.

5 Preheat the air fryer to 350°F/180°C for 3 minutes.

6 Spray spring rolls generously with oil. Carefully place half of the spring rolls in the air-fryer basket; cook for 12 minutes, until golden brown. Transfer to a wire rack. Repeat cooking with remaining spring rolls.

7 Serve spring rolls with cilantro and lime wedges.

SERVE IT Try the spring rolls with the Chili Peanut Dressing on page 75.

prep + cook time
45 minutes makes 10

PICKLE CHIPS
WITH RANCH DIPPING SAUCE

⅓ cup (75g) all-purpose flour
⅔ cup (160ml) buttermilk
1 tbsp hot chili sauce
2¼ cups (170g) panko bread crumbs
1 x 24oz (710g) jar sliced bread and
    butter pickles, drained
olive oil for misting
to serve: sea salt flakes

RANCH DIPPING SAUCE
½ cup (150g) mayonnaise
½ cup (120g) light sour cream
2 tbsp chopped dill
2 tbsp chopped chives
1 small garlic clove, crushed
1 tbsp lemon juice

1 Place flour in a shallow bowl. Lightly beat buttermilk and chili sauce in a second shallow bowl, and place bread crumbs in a third shallow bowl. Dust pickles in flour, shaking off excess, dip in buttermilk mixture, then coat in bread crumbs; spray generously all over with oil.

2 Preheat a 7-quart air fryer to 400°F/200°C for 3 minutes.

3 Carefully place one-third of the pickles in the air-fryer basket in a single layer; cook for 6 minutes, until golden. Transfer to a paper-towel-lined plate. Repeat cooking with remaining pickles.

4 Meanwhile, to make ranch dipping sauce, combine ingredients in a small bowl.

5 Sprinkle pickle chips with sea salt flakes and serve with ranch dipping sauce.

**prep + cook time
40 minutes
serves 6**

FRIES TO FIGHT FOR

GREEK FETA & OREGANO FRIES

prep + cook time 15 minutes serves 4

Preheat a 5.3-quart air fryer to 400°F/200°C for 3 minutes. Place 1½lb (700g) frozen French fries in the air-fryer basket with 8 unpeeled garlic cloves, then spray with oil; cook for 10 minutes, turning halfway through cooking time, or until fries are golden. Tip fries into a large bowl. Crumble over 3½oz (100g) feta and sprinkle with 1 tsp sea salt flakes and 1 tsp dried oregano; toss to combine.

ZUCCHINI FRIES

prep + cook time 30 minutes serves 4

Cut 3 large zucchini in half crosswise. Cut zucchini halves into "fries" ½in (1cm) thick. Combine ⅔ cup (70g) ground almonds (or panko bread crumbs), ½ cup (50g) finely grated Parmesan cheese, 1 tsp each of smoked paprika and finely chopped rosemary or oregano, and a pinch of chili powder in a bowl. Preheat a 5.3-quart air fryer to 400°F/200°C for 3 minutes. Toss zucchini fries with 2 tbsp extra-virgin olive oil, then coat in almond mixture. Place half of the fries in the air-fryer basket in a single layer; cook for 10 minutes, turning halfway through cooking time, until fries are golden. Transfer to a plate; cover to keep warm. Repeat with remaining fries. Season to taste. Serve with Greek Yogurt Dipping Sauce (see recipe right).

HALLOUMI FRIES

prep + cook time 15 minutes serves 4

Cut 2 x 8oz (225g) blocks of Halloumi cheese horizontally into three slices each. Cut each slice into three "fries"; you will have 18 total. Combine ½ cup (75g) all-purpose flour, 1 tsp each of ground cumin and ground coriander, and ½ tsp smoked paprika in a bowl. Preheat a 5.3-quart air fryer to 400°F/200°C for 3 minutes. Spray the air-fryer basket with oil. Spray Halloumi fries with oil, then coat in flour mixture. Place the Halloumi fries in the basket in a single layer; cook for 5 minutes, until fries are golden. Serve with Greek Yogurt Dipping Sauce (see recipe below).

GREEK YOGURT DIPPING SAUCE

prep time 5 minutes makes 1¼ cups

Combine 1¼ cups (350g) Greek-style yogurt, 1 tsp finely grated lemon zest, 1 smashed garlic clove, 2 tbsp finely chopped dill, and 2 tbsp finely chopped mint; season with salt and pepper to taste. Remove the garlic clove when ready to serve.

TIP Use just one herb in the recipe, if you like.

GREEK FETA &
OREGANO FRIES

HALLOUMI FRIES

ZUCCHINI FRIES

GREEK YOGURT
DIPPING SAUCE

ZUCCHINI BALLS
WITH LEMON YOGURT

1½lb (700g) zucchini, coarsely grated
2 tsp coarse salt
1 egg, lightly beaten
½ cup (120g) fresh firm ricotta, crumbled
⅓ cup (25g) finely grated Parmesan cheese
1 cup (100g) packaged bread crumbs
½ cup (15g) finely chopped flat-leaf parsley
3 scallions, thinly sliced
salt and pepper to taste
olive oil for misting
¾ cup (200g) Greek-style yogurt
1 small garlic clove, crushed
2 tsp finely grated lemon zest
1 tbsp lemon juice
to serve: sea salt flakes

1 Place grated zucchini in a colander and sprinkle with salt; let stand for 20 minutes. Using your hands, squeeze zucchini very firmly to remove any excess liquid; transfer to a large bowl.
2 Add egg, ricotta, Parmesan cheese, bread crumbs, parsley, and scallions to a bowl, then season with salt and pepper; stir until well combined. With damp hands, shape heaped tablespoons of zucchini mixture into balls; place on a sheet pan lined with parchment paper. Spray all over with olive oil.
3 Preheat a 7-quart air fryer to 350°F/180°C for 3 minutes. Cut out a 9in (22cm) round from a piece of parchment paper.
4 Carefully line the air-fryer basket with the parchment paper round. Place zucchini balls in the basket; cook for 25 minutes, turning after 15 minutes of cooking time, until golden and cooked through.
5 Meanwhile, to make lemon yogurt, combine remaining ingredients in a small bowl.
6 Sprinkle zucchini balls with sea salt flakes and serve with lemon yogurt.

**prep + cook time
45 minutes (+ standing)
makes 24**

CRISPY PEPPERONI-FLAVORED PEAS & BEANS

2 x 15oz (425g) cans chickpeas, drained and rinsed
6½oz (200g) frozen edamame beans, thawed
⅓ cup (80ml) extra-virgin olive oil
2 tsp garlic granules (see tip)
2 tsp fennel seeds
2 tsp dried chili flakes
2 tsp onion powder
2 tsp smoked paprika
1 tsp sea salt flakes
¼ cup (50g) pepitas (optional)

1 Preheat a 5.3-quart air fryer to 350°F/180°C for 3 minutes.

2 Place chickpeas on a sheet pan lined with paper towels; pat with more paper towels until well dried. Repeat with edamame beans on fresh paper towels.

3 Toss chickpeas with 2 tablespoons of the olive oil in a large bowl. Combine garlic granules, fennel seeds, chili flakes, onion powder, paprika, and salt flakes in a small bowl. Sprinkle half of the spice mix over chickpeas.

4 Carefully place the chickpeas in the air-fryer basket; cook for 15 minutes, turning twice during cooking time, or until crisp and golden. Add the pepitas, if desired, 2 minutes before the end of cooking time. Transfer to a clean bowl to cool.

5 Combine edamame beans, remaining olive oil, and remaining spice mix in a bowl. Place edamame be in the air-fryer basket; cook for 12 minutes, turning twice during cooking time, or until crisp and darkened. Transfer edamame to bowl with chickpeas to cool.

KEEP IT Crisp peas and beans mixture will keep in an airtight container for up to 1 week.

prep + cook time
40 minutes
makes 3 cups

TIP Garlic granules, sometimes sold as granulated garlic, are sold in small packets or jars alongside other spices in the supermarket.

BACON & LEEK FRITTATAS

1 tbsp extra-virgin olive oil
3 slices thick-cut bacon, finely
   chopped
½ small leek, thinly sliced
2 eggs
⅓ cup (80ml) light cream
salt and pepper to taste
2 tbsp grated mozzarella cheese
1 tbsp grated Cheddar cheese
1 tbsp grated Parmesan cheese
to serve: sea salt flakes (optional)

1 Grease a 12-cup (1 tbsp/20ml) mini muffin pan.

2 Heat oil in a medium skillet; cook bacon, stirring, for 3 minutes or until lightly browned. Add leek; cook, stirring, for 5 minutes or until leek softens and bacon is crisp. Let cool for 2 minutes.

3 Preheat a 7-quart air fryer to 350°F/180°C for 3 minutes.

4 Spoon bacon mixture into muffin pan cups. Lightly whisk eggs and cream in a bowl, then season with salt and pepper. Combine the three cheeses in a small bowl; stir 2 tablespoons of the cheese into the egg mixture. Pour mixture into muffin pan cups; sprinkle with remaining cheese.

5 Gently lower muffin pan into the air-fryer basket; cook for 5 minutes. Cover pan with greased foil; cook for a further 5 minutes until frittatas are golden and cooked through. Remove muffin pan from the air fryer. Leave frittatas in pan for 5 minutes before turning, top-side up, onto a wire rack to cool.

6 Sprinkle frittatas with sea salt flakes, if desired, to serve.

**prep + cook time
30 minutes
makes 12**

SRIRACHA VEGETABLE TEMPURA

1 bunch of asparagus
1 head of broccoli
1 medium carrot
4½oz (150g) oyster mushrooms
⅔ cup (100g) all-purpose flour
½ tsp fine salt
1 egg
1 tbsp sriracha chili sauce
¾ cup (180ml) chilled club soda
2¼ cups (185g) panko bread crumbs
⅓ cup (100ml) extra-virgin olive oil
to serve: tamari or ponzu sauce,
    finely chopped red chili pepper,
    and toasted sesame seeds

1 Trim asparagus. Cut broccoli into florets. Cut carrot into ¼in (5mm) slices on a diagonal. Separate mushrooms, if needed.

2 Combine flour and salt in a large bowl. Place egg, sriracha, and club soda in a bowl; whisk to combine. Add egg mixture to flour mixture; whisk until just combined.

3 Preheat a 5.3-quart air fryer to 350°F/180°C for 3 minutes. Line a sheet pan with parchment paper and top a second sheet pan with a wire rack.

4 Place bread crumbs in a bowl; drizzle over oil. Using your fingertips, rub the oil into the crumbs until well combined. Working with one vegetable piece at a time, dip in batter, allowing excess to drip off, then coat in bread crumb mixture; place on lined baking sheet. Continue coating until you have 6–8 vegetable pieces ready to cook.

5 Carefully place the vegetables in the air-fryer basket in a single layer; cook for 5 minutes, turning halfway through cooking time, or until golden brown. Transfer to the wire rack over the second sheet pan.

6 Repeat coating and cooking remaining vegetable pieces in four more batches.

7 Serve vegetable tempura with tamari sprinkled with finely chopped red chili and toasted sesame seeds.

prep + cook time
40 minutes
serves 4

DRIED
WATERMELON

DRIED PINEAPPLE

DRIED APPLE

DRIED KIWIFRUIT

DRIED PINEAPPLE

Lightly spray two of the included racks of an 11-quart air fryer with olive oil. Cut a pineapple in half crosswise through the middle (reserve the other half for another use). Peel, then remove the core with an apple corer. Thinly slice pineapple into ¼in (2mm) thick rings. Arrange rings over racks in a single layer. Carefully place the racks in the air fryer. Set air fryer to dehydration setting and set temperature to 160°F/70°C; cook for 4 hours, rotating racks halfway through cooking time, or until pineapple is dried. Remove racks from the air fryer. Leave pineapple on racks to cool. Store in an airtight container in a cool, dry place for up to 2 weeks.

DRIED APPLE

Lightly spray two of the included racks of an 11-quart air fryer with olive oil. Using a mandolin or V-slicer, thinly slice 2 red apples into slices ⅛in (1mm) thick. Arrange apple slices over racks in a single layer. Carefully place the racks in the air fryer. Set air fryer to dehydration setting and set temperature to 160°F/70°C; cook for 4 hours, rotating racks halfway through cooking time, or until apple is dried and crisp. Remove racks from the air fryer. Leave apple on racks to cool. Store in an airtight container in a cool, dry place for up to 2 weeks.

4 WAYS

DEHYDRATED SNACKS

DRIED WATERMELON

Lightly spray two of the included racks of an 11-quart air fryer with olive oil. Using a sharp knife, cut an 1¾lb (800g) wedge of watermelon into slices ¼in (2mm) thick. Arrange watermelon slices over racks in a single layer. Carefully place the racks in the air fryer. Set air fryer to dehydration setting and set temperature to 160°F/70°C; cook for 4 hours, rotating racks halfway through cooking time, or until watermelon is dried. Remove racks from the air fryer. Leave watermelon on racks to cool. Store in an airtight container in a cool, dry place for up to 2 weeks.

DRIED KIWI FRUIT

Lightly spray two of the included racks of an 11-quart air fryer with olive oil. Peel 4 kiwifruit, then thinly slice into ¼in (2mm) thick slices. Arrange kiwifruit slices over racks in a single layer. Carefully place the racks in the air fryer. Set air fryer to dehydration setting and set temperature to 160°F/70°C; cook for 4 hours, rotating racks halfway through cooking time, or until kiwifruit is dried. Remove racks from the air fryer. Leave kiwifruit on racks to cool. Store in an airtight container in a cool, dry place for up to 2 weeks.

prep + cook time
4 hours 15 minutes
(+ cooling)

SPINACH & FETA TWISTS

8oz (250g) frozen spinach, thawed
2 sheets of frozen puff pastry, thawed
3½oz (100g) feta, crumbled
½ cup (40g) finely grated Parmesan cheese
oil for misting

1 Place spinach in a fine sieve; squeeze out excess liquid. Coarsely chop spinach, then pat dry between sheets of paper towels.
2 Place a pastry sheet on a sheet pan lined with parchment paper. Top with half of the spinach, half of the combined cheeses, then the remaining sheet of pastry; sprinkle over remaining spinach and cheeses. Cut pastry stack in half; place one half on top of the other half and press down firmly. Place pastry stack in the freezer for 5 minutes to firm, then cut crosswise into 24 strips. Pinch one end of a strip, then twist from that end to the other end until 8in (20cm) long; pinch other end to seal. Repeat twisting with remaining strips.

3 Preheat a 5.3-quart air fryer to 400°F/200°C for 3 minutes.
4 Spray the air-fryer basket with oil. Carefully place half of the twists in the basket; cook for 5 minutes, until golden brown and cooked through. Transfer to a wire rack to cool. Repeat cooking with remaining twists.

KEEP IT Twists will keep in an airtight container for up to 3 days.

**prep + cook time
30 minutes
makes 24**

VEGGIE CHIPS

3 large orange carrots
3 medium purple carrots
3 medium parsnips
1 medium beet
extra-virgin olive oil for misting
to serve: sea salt flakes

SWAP IT
Get crisping with other veggies: try sweet potato and celery root. Celery root pops up around winter and looks rather unimpressive, but don't let that put you off—it tastes amazing.

1 Preheat a 5.3-quart air fryer to 250°F/120°C for 3 minutes.

2 Cut carrots, parsnips, and beet in half lengthwise. Using a mandolin or V-slicer, slice vegetables, cut-side down, into ¼in (2mm) thick slices.

3 Carefully place purple carrot and beet slices in the air-fryer basket; cook for 30 minutes, stirring halfway through cooking time and separating the slices, or until crisp. Transfer purple carrot chips to a sheet pan; cover to keep warm. Cook beet chips for a further 5 minutes; transfer to pan with purple carrot chips. Spray chips with olive oil and sprinkle with sea salt flakes. Let cool.

4 Repeat cooking with parsnip slices, then orange carrot slices, cooking at 250°F/120°C for 25 minutes each. Add to tray with purple carrot and beet chips; spray with oil and sprinkle with more sea salt flakes or one of the seasoning variations below.

SEASONING VARIATIONS
fennel & chili Using a mortar and pestle, crush 2 teaspoons fennel seeds until coarsely ground; stir in 1 teaspoon dried chili flakes until evenly mixed.

sumac & thyme Combine 1 teaspoon sumac and 2 teaspoons chopped thyme.

smoked paprika Combine 1 teaspoon smoked paprika and 1 teaspoon onion powder.

KEEP IT Veggie chips will keep in an airtight container for up to 4 days.

prep + cook time 1¾ hours
serves 6

PEAR & RICOTTA FRITTERS

¼ cup (60ml) buttermilk
1 egg
½ cup (125g) smooth ricotta
2 tbsp sugar
½ tsp ground cinnamon
¾ cup (105g) all-purpose flour
½ teaspoon baking powder
1 large, bosc pear, peeled and grated
olive oil for misting
1 cup (280g) vanilla yogurt
2 tbsp honey

1 Preheat a 7-quart air fryer to 400°F/200°C for 3 minutes.
2 Whisk the buttermilk, egg, ricotta, sugar, and cinnamon in a medium bowl until well combined. Sift flour and baking powder together then sift over ricotta mixture; mix to combine. Fold in pear.
3 Carefully line the air-fryer basket with parchment paper. Drop 6 heaped tablespoons of fritter mixture onto the parchment about ¾in (2cm) apart. Using the back of a spoon, smooth the surface of the fritters to flatten slightly, then spray with olive oil; cook for 8 minutes, turning halfway through cooking time, until golden and cooked through. Transfer to a plate; cover loosely with foil to keep warm. Repeat cooking with remaining fritter mixture and olive oil to make 12 fritters in total.
4 Serve fritters warm, dolloped with yogurt and drizzled with honey.

prep + cook time
30 minutes
makes 12

FAVORITE DINNERS

When you have a family to feed or are ravenous after arriving home from work, getting a meal on the table fast is the priority. The air fryer, with its fast heating and rapid air circulation, makes this possible.

BACON 'N' CHEESE BURGERS

1lb (450g) ground beef
1 egg
¾ cup (75g) panko bread crumbs
2 tbsp barbecue sauce
1 tsp smoked paprika
1 garlic clove, crushed
¼ cup (70g) ketchup
salt and pepper to taste
olive oil for misting
4 slices of Cheddar cheese
4 slices thick-cut bacon
4 large brioche buns
2 tbsp mayonnaise
4 Little Gem lettuce leaves
⅓ cup (40g) burger pickles
to serve: sweet potato fries

1 Using your hands, combine beef, egg, bread crumbs, barbecue sauce, paprika, garlic, and 1 tablespoon of the ketchup in a large bowl, then season with salt and pepper; mix well. Shape mixture into four patties the same size as the brioche buns; ensure they will all fit in the air-fryer basket. Spray all over with olive oil.

2 Preheat a 7-quart air fryer to 350°F/180°C for 3 minutes.

3 Spray the air-fryer basket with olive oil. Carefully arrange patties in the basket; cook for 10 minutes, turning halfway through cooking time, or until browned and cooked through. Transfer to a plate and top each with a slice of Cheddar cheese; cover loosely with foil to keep warm.

4 Carefully arrange the bacon in the air-fryer basket. Reset the temperature to 400°F/200°C; cook for 5 minutes until crisp.

5 Split and toast brioche buns. Spread bun bases with mayonnaise, then top with lettuce, patties, bacon, pickles, and remaining ketchup; sandwich together with bun tops.

6 Serve burgers with sweet potato fries.

**prep + cook time
30 minutes
serves 4**

SWEET POTATO PARMIGIANA

4 sweet potatoes, scrubbed
2 tbsp extra-virgin olive oil
salt and pepper to taste
⅓ cup (85g) pasta sauce
4oz (125g) shaved ham
⅔ cup (70g) coarsely grated
   mozzarella cheese
2 tbsp finely grated Parmesan
   cheese
to serve: extra finely grated
   Parmesan cheese and basil leaves

1 Pierce sweet potatoes all over with a small, sharp knife or fork; rub with oil and season with salt and pepper. Wrap each sweet potato individually in foil.
2 Preheat a 7-quart air fryer to 400°F/200°C for 3 minutes.
3 Carefully place sweet potatoes in the air-fryer basket in a single layer; cook for 50 minutes, turning halfway through cooking time, or until tender. Transfer to a plate; remove and discard foil.
4 Cut sweet potatoes in half lengthwise, being careful not to cut all the way through; open out so that the flesh sides are facing up. Spoon over pasta sauce, then top with ham and cheeses.
5 Carefully place topped sweet potatoes in the air-fryer basket in a single layer; cook for 5 minutes or until cheese topping is golden and melted.
6 Serve each sweet potato parmigiana topped with extra finely grated Parmesan cheese and basil leaves.

prep + cook time
1 hour 10 minutes
serves 4

MATCH IT Italian-style Rice Salad, page 98.

BEEF SKEWERS
WITH GARLIC TZATZIKI

You will need 8 x 9in (22cm)
   metal skewers for this recipe.
1 tbsp finely grated lemon zest
2 tbsp lemon juice
1 tsp dried oregano
1 tbsp extra-virgin olive oil
3 garlic cloves, crushed
1lb (450g) rib-eye steak, cut into 1in
   (2.5cm) pieces
1 medium red bell pepper, seeded
   and cut into 1¼in (3cm) pieces
1 medium yellow bell pepper,
   seeded and cut into 1¼in (3cm)
   pieces
7oz (220g) tub tzatziki (see tips)
to serve: salad leaves and
   lemon wedges

1 Combine lemon zest and juice, oregano, oil and two-thirds of the garlic in a shallow dish; add steak and toss to coat. Thread steak and both peppers, alternately, onto skewers.
2 Preheat a 7-quart air fryer to 400°F/200°C for 3 minutes.
3 Carefully, place skewers in the air-fryer basket; cook for 8 minutes, turning halfway through cooking time, for medium or until cooked to your liking.
4 Meanwhile, stir remaining garlic into tzatziki in the tub; transfer to a serving bowl.
5 Place skewers on a platter. Serve with tzatziki, salad leaves, and lemon wedges.

TIPS If you are using a smaller air fryer, you will need to cook the skewers in batches. For homemade tzatziki, coarsely grate ½ small cucumber and squeeze out the excess liquid; combine in a bowl with ¾ cup (210g) Greek-style yogurt and ½ crushed garlic clove, then season with salt and pepper.

**prep + cook time
30 minutes serves 4**

MATCH IT Greek-style Potatoes, page 145.

JAMAICAN FISH TACOS

1 tsp ground allspice
½ tsp dried thyme
1½ tsp cayenne pepper
1 tsp ground cinnamon
1½ tbsp garlic powder
2 tbsp light soft brown sugar
¼ cup (60ml) olive oil
1¾lb (800g) firm white skinless fish
   fillets, cut into long pieces (see tip)
salt to taste
16 x 5½in (14cm) flour tortillas
oil for misting
to serve: lime wedges

AVOCADO CREAM
2 medium avocados
½ cup (120g) sour cream
2 tbsp lime juice

SLAW
11oz (350g) green cabbage,
   shredded
2 cups (60g) cilantro leaves
1 small red onion, thinly sliced
1 long green chili,
   seeded, thinly sliced

1 Combine allspice, thyme, cayenne pepper, cinnamon, garlic powder, brown sugar and oil in a medium bowl; add fish and toss to coat. Season with salt.

2 To make avocado cream, blend or process ingredients until smooth; season to taste.

3 Wrap tortillas in foil. Place in the basket of a 5.3-quart air fryer; at 350°F/180°C, cook for 5 minutes to preheat the air fryer and warm through the tortillas.

4 Carefully transfer tortillas to a plate; cover to keep warm. Spray fish with oil and place in the air-fryer basket; cook for 8 minutes, turning halfway through cooking time, or until cooked through.

5 Meanwhile, to make slaw, combine ingredients in a bowl.

6 Fill warm tortillas with fish and slaw; top with avocado cream. Serve with lime wedges.

TIP Cut fish fillets lengthwise on the diagonal into ¾in (1.5cm) wide, 4¾in (12cm) long strips.

PREP IT Fish can be prepared to the end of step 1 up to 4 hours ahead. Avocado cream and slaw can also be prepared up to 4 hours ahead. Refrigerate until needed.

prep + cook time
25 minutes serves 8

SWAP IT Replace all the spices with a packet of taco seasoning.

53

COCONUT HONEY SHRIMP

½ cup (75g) all-purpose flour
2 eggs
1½ cups (115g) unsweetened
    shredded coconut
1 cup (75g) panko bread crumbs
1¼lb (600g) peeled uncooked
    shrimp, tails intact
olive oil for misting
to serve: steamed jasmine rice
    and steamed bok choy

HONEY SAUCE
⅓ cup (120g) honey
1 tbsp lemon juice
1 tbsp soy sauce
1 tsp finely grated fresh ginger
1 garlic clove, crushed
½ tsp Chinese five-spice powder
2 tsp cornstarch

1 Place flour in a shallow bowl. Lightly whisk eggs in a second shallow bowl. Combine coconut and bread crumbs in a third shallow bowl. Dust shrimp in flour, shaking off excess, dip in egg, then coat in coconut mixture; place on a sheet pan. Refrigerate for 30 minutes.

2 Meanwhile, to make honey sauce, combine honey, lemon juice, soy sauce, ginger, garlic, and five-spice powder in a small saucepan over a medium heat; cook, stirring, for 2 minutes or until honey melts. Bring to a boil. Blend cornstarch and 1 tablespoon water in a small cup. Whisk cornstarch mixture into sauce; cook, stirring, for 2 minutes or until slightly thickened. Remove from heat; cover to keep warm.

3 Preheat a 7-quart air fryer to 400°F/200°C for 3 minutes.

4 Spray shrimp generously all over with olive oil. Carefully place half of the shrimp in the air-fryer basket in a single layer; cook for 6 minutes, turning halfway through cooking time, until golden and just cooked through. Transfer to a plate; cover loosely with foil to keep warm. Repeat cooking with remaining shrimp.

5 Serve shrimp with steamed rice and steamed bok choy, drizzled with honey sauce.

**prep + cook time
40 minutes
(+ refrigeration)
serves 4**

HERBY LAMB KOFTAS
WITH GREEN TAHINI

1lb (450g) ground lamb
2 tsp ground cumin
2 tsp ground coriander
1 tsp paprika
1 egg, lightly beaten
¼ cup (25g) packaged bread crumbs
½ cup (25g) finely chopped mint
½ cup (15g) finely chopped
   flat-leaf parsley
olive oil for misting
½ cup (140g) Greek-style yogurt
2 tbsp tahini
2 tbsp lemon juice
to serve: grilled pita bread rounds,
   cut into wedges

TOMATO SALAD
8oz (225g) mixed baby
   tomatoes, halved
1 cucumber, thickly sliced
2 tbsp mint leaves
2 tbsp flat-leaf parsley leaves
extra-virgin olive oil, to drizzle
Salt and pepper to taste

1 Using your hands, combine lamb, cumin, coriander, paprika, egg, bread crumbs, and half of each of the chopped mint and parsley in a bowl; mix well. With damp hands, shape level tablespoons of lamb mixture into balls to make koftas; place on a sheet pan. Spray all over with olive oil.

2 Preheat a 7-quart air fryer to 350°F/180°C for 3 minutes.

3 Spray the air-fryer basket with olive oil. Carefully place koftas in the basket in a single layer; cook for 8 minutes, shaking the basket halfway through cooking time, until browned and cooked through.

4 Meanwhile, to make green tahini, combine yogurt, tahini, lemon juice, and remaining chopped mint and parsley in a small bowl.

5 To make tomato salad, combine tomatoes, cucumber, mint, and parsley on a platter; drizzle with oil and season with salt and pepper to taste.

6 Add koftas and green tahini to platter. Serve with grilled pita bread.

prep + cook time
35 minutes serves 4

MATCH IT Lentil Tabbouleh, page 98.

BARBECUE BOURBON CHICKEN WINGS

½ cup (140g) barbecue sauce
¼ cup (60ml) bourbon
1 tbsp Dijon mustard
3lb (1.5kg) chicken wings
to serve: extra barbecue sauce

1 Combine barbecue sauce, bourbon, and mustard in a large bowl; add chicken and toss to coat.
2 Preheat a 7-quart air fryer to 350°F/180°C for 3 minutes.
3 Carefully place chicken in the air-fryer basket; cook for 20 minutes, basting and turning occasionally, or until cooked through.
4 Serve chicken brushed with extra barbecue sauce.

MATCH IT Feta, Dill & Bacon Potatoes, page 145.

prep + cook time
30 minutes serves 4

PICK-A-FLAVOR PIZZA NIGHT

---

1 x 8oz (225g) can refrigerated
  biscuits
⅔ cup (170g) pasta sauce
1 medium red onion, thinly sliced
4 slices thick-cut bacon,
  cooked, crumbled
3½oz (100g) pancetta, torn
5oz (170g) cured chorizo, sliced
10oz (300g) mozzarella cheese,
  sliced
1 small red chili, sliced
to serve: basil leaves

1 Preheat a 5.3-quart air fryer to 350°F/180°C for 3 minutes.

2 Press biscuits into one large ball on a lightly floured work surface. Roll out into a 6½in x 10½in (16cm x 26cm) oval on a piece of parchment paper. Trim parchment paper so that it is 1¼in (3cm) larger all around than the dough base.

3 Spread pizza base with pasta sauce; top with onion, bacon, pancetta, chorizo, mozzarella cheese, and chili pepper (or choose another pizza flavor).

4 Using the parchment paper as an aid, carefully lower the pizza into the air-fryer basket. Reset the temperature to 340°F/170°C; cook for 15 minutes until pizza crust is golden and cooked through.

5 Serve pizza topped with basil leaves.

OTHER FLAVORS

shrimp Omit the meats and mozzarella cheese, and replace with 8 uncooked peeled and deveined shrimp tossed in 2 teaspoons extra-virgin olive oil. Serve topped with arugula and grated lemon zest.

gimme greens Omit the meats and replace with 5½oz (175g) halved tenderstem broccoli stalks and ¼ cup (50g) halved kalamata olives. Serve topped with crumbled goat cheese and grated lemon zest.

eggplant & ricotta Omit the meats and replace with 14½oz (450g) chargrilled eggplant slices and ⅓ cup (100g) ricotta. Serve topped with pesto.

**prep + cook time
25 minutes serves 2**

SALMON FISH CAKES
WITH LEMON & HERBS

3 medium russet potatoes,
  coarsely chopped
2 tbsp olive oil
olive oil for misting
1lb (450g) skinless boneless
  salmon fillets
2 scallions, thinly sliced
2 tsp finely grated lemon zest
1 tbsp finely chopped dill or parsley
1 egg, lightly beaten
1½ cups (110g) panko bread crumbs
salt and pepper to taste
Pick-a-Sauce (see pages 74–75)
to serve: lime wedges

1 Preheat a 5.3-quart air fryer to 350°F/180°C for 3 minutes.

2 Boil, steam, or microwave potatoes until tender; drain. Mash potatoes with olive oil until smooth.

3 Meanwhile, spray the air-fryer basket with olive oil. Carefully place salmon in the basket; cook for 6 minutes until salmon is cooked through. Pull out the air-fryer pan and basket; let salmon cool in the basket.

4 Flake salmon into the mashed potato; mash until salmon breaks into smaller pieces. Add scallions, lemon zest, dill, egg, and half of the bread crumbs, then season with salt and pepper; stir to combine. With damp hands, shape mixture into eight patties; place on a sheet pan, and place in freezer for 10 minutes to firm.

5 Coat patties in remaining bread crumbs; spray generously with olive oil.

6 Place patties in the air-fryer basket; at 350°F/180°C, cook for 8 minutes, turning halfway through cooking time, or until golden and heated through.

7 Serve fish cakes with your choice of Pick-a-Sauce and lime wedges.

SWAP IT To make red curry fish cakes, use the equivalent weight of sweet potatoes instead of russet potatoes and stir 2 tablespoons Thai red curry paste into the mash; use cilantro instead of dill.

**prep + cook time
45 minutes (+ cooling
& freezing)
makes 8**

TIP Short on time? Use a 15oz (475g) tub of mashed potato (or sweet potato) and 9½oz (300g) hot-smoked salmon.

CHICKEN WINGS

4 WAYS

PINEAPPLE HULI-HULI

STICKY SESAME

SMOKY BARBECUE

STICKY POMEGRANATE

CHICKEN WINGS

prep + cook time 50 minutes (+ refrigeration) serves 4

Toss 3lb (1.5kg) chicken wings with chosen marinade below in a large bowl. Refrigerate for 1–2 hours. Preheat air fryer to 350°F/180°C for 3 minutes. Carefully place chicken in the air-fryer basket; cook for 40 minutes, turning occasionally, until chicken is cooked.

STICKY SESAME

Combine 4 thinly sliced scallions, 3 crushed garlic cloves, ¼ cup (60ml) each of soy sauce and Shaohsing rice wine, 3 tsp finely grated fresh ginger, and 2 tbsp light soft brown sugar in a bowl. Serve cooked wings topped with 2 tbsp toasted sesame seeds and extra sliced scallion.

STICKY POMEGRANATE

Combine 1 cup (220g) firmly packed light soft brown sugar, 1½ cups (375ml) pomegranate juice, 3 tsp grated orange zest, 2 crushed garlic cloves, 1½ tbsp each of Worcestershire sauce and Dijon mustard, and ⅓ cup (80ml) ketchup in a saucepan, stirring to mix through evenly. Bring to a boil; stir occasionally over medium heat for 10 minutes or until reduced by half. Serve cooked wings topped with pomegranate seeds.

PINEAPPLE HULI-HULI

Combine ⅓ cup (110g) firmly packed light soft brown sugar, ⅔ cup (170ml) fresh pineapple juice, ½ cup (125ml) each of ketchup and soy sauce, ⅓ cup (80ml) malt vinegar, 1 tbsp finely grated fresh ginger, and 2 crushed garlic cloves in a skillet. Boil over medium heat for 5 minutes. Sprinkle wings with 1 tbsp paprika before tossing in marinade. Serve cooked wings topped with cilantro.

SMOKY BARBECUE

Combine ½ cup (175g) honey, ½ cup (125ml) smoky barbecue sauce, and 2 tbsp teriyaki sauce in a bowl. Serve cooked wings with thinly sliced long red chili pepper and lime wedges.

STUFFED EGGPLANT
WITH LENTILS

2 large eggplants, halved lengthwise
salt and pepper to taste
2 tsp table salt
olive oil for misting
1 tbsp extra-virgin olive oil
1 medium onion, finely chopped
2 garlic cloves, crushed
1 tsp ground cumin
1 tsp smoked paprika
1 x 14oz (400g) can brown lentils,
   drained and rinsed
1 x 12oz (275g) can cherry tomatoes
¼ cup chopped oregano leaves
3½oz (100g) feta, crumbled
⅓ cup (25g) finely grated Parmesan
   cheese
to serve: extra oregano leaves

1 Using a small, sharp knife, score the cut side of eggplant halves in a diamond pattern without cutting all the way through; season with salt. Place, cut-side down, on a wire rack for 30 minutes; rinse and pat dry with a paper towel. Using a teaspoon, carefully scoop out eggplant flesh, leaving a shell ½in (1cm) thick. Finely chop eggplant flesh. Spray eggplant shells with olive oil.

2 Preheat a 7-quart air fryer to 350°F/180°C for 3 minutes.

3 Carefully place eggplant shells, cut-side up, in the air-fryer basket; cook for 12 minutes, until softened.

4 Meanwhile, heat oil in a large skillet over medium-high heat; cook onion, stirring, for 5 minutes or until softened. Add garlic, cumin, and paprika; cook, stirring, for 1 minute or until fragrant. Add eggplant flesh; cook, stirring occasionally, for 5 minutes or until tender. Add lentils and tomatoes; bring to a simmer. Stir in oregano; season with salt and pepper to taste. Let cool for 5 minutes. Stir half of the feta into the lentil mixture.

5 Transfer eggplant shells to a plate. Spoon lentil mixture into the shells, then sprinkle with Parmesan cheese and remaining feta; spray lightly with olive oil.

6 Carefully place stuffed eggplants in the air-fryer basket; cook for 8 minutes until lightly browned and tender.

7 Serve stuffed eggplants sprinkled with extra oregano leaves.

prep + cook time
50 minutes (+ standing)
serves 4

CHICKEN CHIMICHANGAS
WITH AVOCADO SALSA

3 cups (480g) shredded cooked
  chicken
1oz (30g) packet taco seasoning
1 cup (120g) coarsely grated
  Cheddar cheese
6½oz (200g) jar taco sauce
salt and pepper to taste
4 x 8in (20cm) flour tortillas,
  slightly warmed
olive oil for misting
1 medium avocado, diced
1 medium tomato, chopped
½ small red onion, finely chopped
2 tbsp finely chopped cilantro
1 tbsp lime juice
1 tbsp extra-virgin olive oil
2 Little Gem lettuce, torn

1 Combine chicken, taco seasoning, Cheddar cheese, and ⅓ cup (80ml) of the taco sauce in a bowl; season with salt and pepper to taste. Divide chicken mixture among tortillas, placing along the center of each one; flatten chicken mixture slightly and shape into a rectangle. Fold in ends of tortillas, then roll up to enclose the filling; spray all over with olive oil.

2 Preheat a 7-quart air fryer to 350°F/180°C for 3 minutes.

3 Carefully place chimichangas, seam-side down, in the air-fryer basket; cook for 12 minutes, turning halfway through cooking time, until golden and filling is hot.

4 Meanwhile, to make avocado salsa, combine avocado, tomato, onion, cilantro, lime juice, and oil in a bowl; season with salt and pepper.

5 To serve, divide the chimichangas, lettuce, and avocado salsa among plates; drizzle chimichangas with remaining taco sauce.

**prep + cook time
45 minutes
serves 4**

CRISP-SKINNED SALMON
WITH SALSA VERDE

---

4 x 6oz (185g) boneless salmon
    fillets, skin on
1 tbsp extra-virgin olive oil
2 tsp sea salt flakes
1 small shallot, finely chopped
1 garlic clove, crushed
2 tsp finely grated lemon zest
2 tbsp lemon juice
2 tbsp finely chopped dill
¼ cup (10g) chopped
    flat-leaf parsley
2 tbsp chopped chives
1 tbsp capers, coarsely chopped
salt and pepper to taste
to serve: extra sea salt flakes

1 Preheat a 7-quart air fryer to 400°F/200°C for 3 minutes.

2 Rub salmon with oil, then sprinkle with sea salt flakes.

3 Carefully line the air-fryer basket with a silicone mat, if available (see page 11). Place salmon, skin-side up, in the basket; cook for 8 minutes until skin is crisp and salmon is cooked to your liking.

4 Meanwhile, to make salsa verde, combine remaining ingredients in a medium bowl, then season with salt and pepper; mix well.

5 Serve salmon topped with salsa verde and sprinkled with extra sea salt flakes.

MATCH IT Mustard & Mint Potatoes, page 145.

**prep + cook time
25 minutes serves 4**

PEPPERONI CALZONES

1 x 6oz (170g) package sliced pepperoni
1 medium red bell pepper, seeded, thinly sliced
8oz (225g) frozen chopped spinach, thawed
⅓ cup (50g) sun-dried tomato strips, without oil
2 tbsp chopped oregano
⅔ cup (70g) coarsely grated mozzarella cheese
1lb (450g) premade pizza dough
¼ cup (65g) pizza sauce
to serve: sea salt flakes

1 Heat a large nonstick skillet over medium-high heat; cook red bell pepper, stirring, for 5 minutes or until golden and tender. Transfer to a plate lined with paper towels to cool.
2 Meanwhile, squeeze spinach to remove any excess liquid; transfer to a medium bowl. Add pepperoni, red bell pepper, sun-dried tomato strips, oregano, and mozzarella cheese; stir to combine.
3 Divide the pizza dough into 4 pieces. Roll out dough portions on a piece of lightly floured parchment paper into 7¼in (18cm) rounds. Spread dough rounds evenly with pizza sauce, leaving a ¾in (1.5cm) border around the edge. Top half of each dough round with pepperoni filling mixture, then fold dough over to enclose filling; pinch edges to seal, then fold edges over themselves to pleat. Using a small, sharp knife, make three cuts in the tops. Trim the parchment paper so that it is 1¼in (3cm) larger all around than two of the calzones together.
4 Preheat a 7-quart air fryer to 350°F/180°C for 3 minutes.
5 Using the parchment as an aid, carefully lower the two calzones into the air-fryer basket; cook for 14 minutes, turning halfway through cooking time, or until crust is golden and calzones are cooked through. Transfer to a plate; cover to keep warm. Repeat cooking with remaining calzones.
6 Sprinkle calzones with sea salt flakes to serve.

**prep + cook time
45 minutes serves 4**

PICK-A-SAUCE

GREEN OLIVE DRESSING

prep time 5 minutes makes ¾ cup (185ml)
Blend or process ½ cup pitted Sicilian green olives, 2 tbsp
oregano leaves, and ⅓ cup (80ml) olive oil until almost
smooth; season with salt and pepper to taste.

FETA DRESSING

prep time 5 minutes makes 1 cup (250ml)
Blend or process ½ cup (130g) Greek-style yogurt, 3½oz
(100g) crumbled feta, and 2 tbsp lime juice until smooth;
season with salt and pepper to taste. Stir in 1 tsp finely grated
lime zest.

MISO AVOCADO DRESSING

prep time 5 minutes makes ¾ cup (185ml)
Blend or process 1 chopped medium avocado, 3 tsp white
miso paste, and ¼ cup (75g) mayonnaise until smooth;
season with salt and pepper to taste.

CHILI & LIME MAYO

prep time 5 minutes makes about 1½ cups (325g)
Combine 1 cup (235g) mayonnaise with ¼ cup (60ml)
sriracha sauce and 2 tbsp lime juice in a small bowl.

CHILI PEANUT DRESSING

prep time 10 minutes makes ¾ cup (185ml)
Blend or process 1 crushed garlic clove, 1 finely chopped long
red chili, ⅓ cup (50g) roasted unsalted peanuts, ¼ cup (60ml)
fresh lime juice, the roots from 1 bunch of cilantro, 2 tbsp light
soft brown sugar, 1 tbsp soy sauce, and 1 tbsp water until
peanuts are finely chopped and ingredients are combined.

CHIMICHURRI

prep time 5 minutes makes 1¼ cups (310ml)
Blend or process 2 tbsp red wine vinegar, ½ cup (125ml)
extra-virgin olive oil, 4 finely chopped garlic cloves, ½ tsp
dried chili flakes, 1 tsp sea salt flakes, 2 cups (40g) flat-leaf
parsley leaves, and 2 tbsp oregano leaves until finely chopped.

ITALIAN CHICKEN RISSOLES

1lb (450g) ground chicken
1 egg
2 tbsp pine nuts, lightly toasted
¼ cup (15g) finely chopped basil
1 garlic clove, crushed
2oz (60g) sun-dried tomatoes,
    chopped
1 cup (75g) panko bread crumbs
salt and pepper to taste
8 thin slices of prosciutto,
    halved lengthwise
olive oil for misting
1 bunch arugula, trimmed
1 tbsp extra-virgin olive oil
1 tbsp balsamic vinegar
2 tbsp shaved Parmesan cheese

1 Combine chicken, egg, pine nuts, basil, garlic, sun-dried tomatoes, and half of the bread crumbs in a medium bowl, then season with salt and pepper; mix well. Shape mixture into eight ¾in (2cm) thick rissoles. Roll rissoles in remaining bread crumbs to coat lightly. Wrap one strip of prosciutto around each rissole, then another to make a cross shape, twisting ends to secure; lightly spray all over with olive oil.
2 Preheat a 7-quart air fryer to 350°F/180°C for 3 minutes.
3 Spray the air-fryer basket with olive oil. Carefully place the rissoles in the basket; cook for 8 minutes, turning halfway through cooking time, or until browned and cooked through.
4 Meanwhile, place arugula, oil, vinegar, and Parmesan cheese in a medium bowl; toss gently to combine.
5 Serve rissoles with arugula salad.

**prep + cook time
30 minutes serves 4**

SPICED SHRIMP PO' BOYS

2 eggs
1 tbsp water
¾ cup (55g) panko bread crumbs
1 tbsp Cajun seasoning
16 raw shrimp, peeled, deveined
olive oil for misting
1 long baguette
⅓ cup (100g) mayonnaise
1 Little Gem lettuce, leaves
    separated
2 medium tomatoes, thinly sliced
3 gherkins, cut into rounds
to serve: extra mayonnaise, chopped
    chives, and extra gherkins

1 Lightly beat eggs and water in a shallow bowl. Combine bread crumbs and Cajun seasoning in a second shallow bowl. Dip shrimp in egg, then coat in bread crumb mixture; spray generously all over with olive oil.

2 Preheat a 7-quart air fryer to 350°F/180°C for 3 minutes.

3 Carefully place shrimp in the air-fryer basket in a single layer; cook for 6 minutes, turning halfway through cooking time, until golden brown and cooked through.

4 Trim ends from baguette and discard; cut baguette into four even pieces, then split horizontally, being careful not to cut all the way through. Spread bases with mayonnaise, then fill with lettuce, tomato, gherkins, and shrimp; drizzle with extra mayonnaise and sprinkle over chopped chives. Serve with extra gherkins.

**prep + cook time
35 minutes serves 4**

CLASSIC MEATBALLS

2 slices of white bread
⅓ cup (80ml) milk
1 medium onion, coarsely grated
2 garlic cloves, crushed
1 medium carrot, finely grated
1½lb (750g) ground beef
¼ cup (7g) chopped flat-leaf parsley
1 egg, lightly beaten
2 tbsp tomato paste
salt and pepper to taste
olive oil for misting
1½ cups (420g) tomato sauce
12½oz (400g) jar of pasta sauce with olives
to serve: lasagnette (or spaghetti), grated Parmesan cheese, and basil leaves

1 Tear bread into a large bowl; pour over milk. Add onion, garlic, carrot, beef, parsley, egg, and tomato paste; season well. Let stand for 10 minutes without stirring.

2 Preheat a 5.3-quart air fryer to 400°F/200°C for 5 minutes.

3 Using your hands, combine ingredients well in the bowl. With damp hands, shape 1½ tablespoons of the beef mixture into balls; spray with olive oil.

4 Spray the air-fryer basket with olive oil. Carefully place half of the meatballs in the basket in a single layer; cook for 10 minutes, shaking basket halfway through cooking time, until browned and cooked through. Transfer to a tray; cover to keep warm. Repeat cooking with remaining meatballs.

5 Combine tomato sauce and pasta sauce in a bowl. Roll meatballs in tomato sauce mixture; place in a 6in x 8¾in (15cm x 22cm), 1.5-quart oval heatproof dish. Pour remaining tomato sauce mixture over meatballs. Place dish in the basket; cook for 10 minutes, until heated through.

6 Serve meatballs and sauce with pasta, grated Parmesan cheese, and basil leaves.

OTHER FLAVORS

Greek lamb meatballs
Swap ground beef for ground lamb and parsley for oregano. Add 2 teaspoons ground cinnamon and ½ teaspoon chili flakes to tomato sauce mixture in step 5. Serve with orzo, Greek-style yogurt, and pine nuts.

Mexican stuffed meatballs Add 2 teaspoons ground cumin and 1 teaspoon Tabasco sauce to meatball mixture in step 1. Combine 4½oz (150g) each of grated mozzarella and Cheddar cheese; roll into small balls and press into the center of each meatball in step 3.

prep + cook time
45 minutes serves 6

PREP IT The chicken can be prepared to the end of step 2 up to 4 hours ahead; refrigerate until needed.

BREADED CHICKEN
WITH SPICY MAYO

½ cup (75g) all-purpose flour
salt and pepper to taste
2 eggs
1 cup (75g) panko bread crumbs
½ cup (40g) finely grated Parmesan
  cheese
¼ cup (7g) coarsely chopped
  flat-leaf parsley
2 tsp finely grated lemon zest
12 boneless skinless chicken
  tenders (900g)
olive oil for misting
3 cups (75g) mixed salad greens
2 tsp lemon juice
to serve: lemon wedges

SPICY MAYO
⅔ cup (200g) mayonnaise
¾ tsp peri-peri seasoning
2 tsp lemon juice

1 Preheat a 5.3-quart air fryer to 350°F/180°C for 3 minutes.
2 Place flour in a shallow bowl; season with salt and freshly ground black pepper. Lightly beat eggs in a second shallow bowl. Combine bread crumbs, Parmesan cheese, parsley, and lemon zest in a third shallow bowl. Dust chicken in flour, shaking off excess, dip in egg, then coat in bread crumb mixture; spray generously with olive oil.
3 Carefully place chicken in the air-fryer basket; cook for 8 minutes, turning halfway through cooking time, or until golden and cooked through.

4 Meanwhile, to make spicy mayo, combine ingredients in a small bowl.
5 Place salad greens in a medium bowl with lemon juice; toss to combine.
6 Serve breaded chicken with spicy mayo, salad greens, and lemon wedges.

prep + cook time
25 minutes serves 4

LEMON & GARLIC ROAST CHICKEN

4 tbsp (60g) butter, softened
1 garlic clove, crushed
1 tsp sweet paprika
2 tsp chopped rosemary
1 tsp chopped thyme
1 whole chicken, about 2½lb (1.2kg)
½ medium lemon, halved
8 sprigs of lemon thyme
oil for misting
1 garlic bulb, halved crosswise
4 sprigs of bay leaves
1 cup (250ml) gravy, warmed

1 Preheat a 5.3-quart air fryer to 325°F/160°C for 3 minutes.
2 Combine butter, garlic, paprika, rosemary, and thyme in a small bowl.
3 Remove and discard any fat from cavity of chicken. Pat the cavity and skin dry with a paper towel. Tuck wings under body. Run your fingers carefully between the skin and the breast meat. Push butter mixture under skin to cover breast. Fill cavity of chicken with lemon and half of the lemon thyme sprigs. Tie legs together with kitchen twine.
4 Spray the air-fryer basket with oil. Carefully place chicken in the basket and cover loosely with foil; cook for 30 minutes.

5 Uncover chicken and place garlic bulb halves and bay leaves beside it; cook for a further 30 minutes, until juices run clear when a skewer is inserted into the thickest part of a thigh. Transfer chicken, garlic, and bay leaves to a serving dish or platter; let stand for 10 minutes.
6 Serve chicken with the bay leaves, garlic, remaining lemon thyme sprigs, and warm gravy.

**prep + cook time
1¼ hours serves 4**

PREP IT Patties can be prepared a day ahead; refrigerate until needed. Brush with barbecue sauce before cooking.

LOADED KOREAN BURGER
WITH KIMCHI SLAW

1 tbsp light soft brown sugar
2 tbsp soy sauce
¼ cup (85g) gochujang chili paste (see tips)
2 garlic cloves, crushed
2 tsp finely grated fresh ginger
1½lb (700g) ground beef
1 egg
¾ cup (75g) packaged bread crumbs
2 tbsp barbecue sauce
oil for misting
4 slices Cheddar cheese
4 large brioche buns
⅓ cup (100g) Japanese mayonnaise
to serve: sweet potato fries

KIMCHI SLAW
¼ cup (25g) kimchi, finely shredded
2 tsp rice wine vinegar
2 tsp vegetable oil
2 tsp sesame oil
2 cups (160g) shredded cabbage (see tips)
⅓ cup (7g) mint leaves

1 Preheat a 5.3-quart air fryer to 350°F/180°C for 3 minutes.
2 Combine sugar, soy sauce, all but 1 teaspoon of the chili paste, garlic, and ginger in a bowl. Add beef, egg, and bread crumbs; using your hands, combine well. Shape mixture into four patties the same size as the brioche buns; ensure that they will all fit in the air-fryer basket. Brush all over with barbecue sauce.
3 Spray the air-fryer basket with oil. Carefully place patties in the basket; cook for 6 minutes, turning halfway through cooking time, or until browned and cooked through. Top each patty with a slice of Cheddar cheese. Slide air-fryer pan and basket back into appliance. With air fryer turned off, leave patties for 1 minute for cheese to melt.
4 Meanwhile, to make kimchi slaw, combine kimchi, vinegar, and oils in a large bowl. Add cabbage and mint to bowl; toss to combine.
5 Split and toast brioche buns. Spread bases with combined mayonnaise and remaining 1 teaspoon chili paste, then top with patties and slaw; sandwich together with bun tops.
6 Serve burgers with sweet potato fries.

TIPS Gochujang is a Korean fermented red chili paste, available in major supermarkets and Asian grocers. Substitute with your favorite chili sauce, if you like, adjusting the amount to your heat tolerance and palate. We used a mix of shredded red cabbage and napa cabbage; however, you can use any cabbage mix you like, including undressed coleslaw-type mixes.

prep + cook time
30 minutes makes 4

PORTUGUESE CHICKEN DRUMSTICKS

2 garlic cloves, chopped
1 long red chili pepper, chopped
1 tbsp finely chopped oregano
2 tbsp apple cider vinegar
1 tbsp extra-virgin olive oil
1 tbsp light soft brown sugar
2 tsp smoked paprika
1 tsp sea salt flakes
8 chicken drumsticks (2½lb/1.2kg)

1 To make marinade, place garlic, chili, and oregano in a small food processor or blender; blend until finely chopped. Add vinegar, oil, sugar, paprika, and salt; process until combined.

2 Place chicken in a large shallow dish; add marinade and toss to coat. Cover with plastic wrap. Refrigerate for 2 hours.

3 Preheat a 7-quart air fryer to 400°F/200°C for 3 minutes.

4 Carefully place drained chicken (see tip, right) in the air-fryer basket; cook for 25 minutes, turning halfway through cooking time, or until cooked through.

TIP Heat drained marinade in a small saucepan for 3 minutes until reduced and slightly thickened, then use to baste the chicken while cooking.

**prep + cook time
40 minutes
(+ refrigeration)
serves 4**

VEGGIES & SIDES

The air fryer can make your side dishes the stars of the meal. Think warm veggie salads, baked potatoes, loaded corn, mac 'n' cheese croquettes, crisp tofu with Asian-style dressing, carrot rösti, and more.

CAJUN SWEET POTATO WEDGES

2 tsp ground cumin
1 tsp ground coriander
1 tsp garlic salt
½ tsp smoked paprika
½ tsp dried thyme
½ tsp dried oregano
½ tsp cayenne pepper
2lb (1kg) small sweet potatoes
1 tbsp extra-virgin olive oil
to serve: sea salt flakes,
   chopped cilantro,
   and sour cream

1 Preheat a 7-quart air fryer to 400°F/200°C for 3 minutes.
2 To make Cajun spice mix, combine cumin, coriander, garlic salt, paprika, thyme, oregano, and cayenne pepper in a small bowl.
3 Scrub sweet potatoes and pat dry; cut into long, thin wedges. Place in a large bowl with oil and the Cajun spice mix; toss to coat evenly.
4 Carefully place wedges in the air-fryer basket; cook for 15 minutes, turning halfway through cooking time, or until golden and cooked through.

5 Sprinkle wedges with sea salt flakes and chopped cilantro. Serve with sour cream.

**prep + cook time
25 minutes serves 4**

MAPLE-ROASTED CARROTS
WITH HAZELNUTS

1 lb (450g) mixed color baby carrots, peeled
2 tbsp (30g) butter, melted
1 tbsp extra-virgin olive oil
2 tbsp maple syrup
1 garlic clove, crushed
salt and pepper to taste
¼ cup (35g) raw hazelnuts

1 Preheat a 7-quart air fryer to 400°F/200°C for 3 minutes.
2 Cut any large carrots in half lengthwise. Place carrots in a large bowl with butter, oil, maple syrup, and garlic, then season with salt and freshly ground black pepper; toss to combine.
3 Carefully place carrots in the air-fryer basket, reserving any leftover butter mixture in the bowl; cook for 10 minutes, turning halfway through cooking time.

4 Sprinkle hazelnuts over carrots; cook for a further 5 minutes or until carrots are golden and tender.
5 To serve, drizzle carrots and hazelnuts with reserved butter mixture.

prep + cook time
25 minutes serves 4

SALT 'N' VINEGAR
SMASHED
POTATOES

2½lb (1.2kg) red potatoes,
   halved if large
3 cups (750ml) white vinegar
1 tbsp cooking salt
¼ cup (60ml) extra-virgin olive oil
1 garlic bulb, cloves separated
   but unpeeled
1 bunch (20g) rosemary sprigs
sea salt to taste

1 Place potatoes in a large saucepan. Add vinegar, cooking salt, and enough water to just cover; bring to a boil. Boil, partially covered, for 15–20 minutes (the cooking time will vary depending on the size of the potatoes) or until potatoes are tender; drain.

2 Preheat a 5.3-quart air fryer to 400°F/200°C for 3 minutes.

3 Transfer potatoes to a large sheet pan. Using a potato masher or the back of a spoon, press down on potatoes until flattened slightly and skins split. Brush potatoes with oil.

4 Carefully place potatoes in the air-fryer basket; cook for 30 minutes, turning twice during cooking time, or until potatoes are golden. Add garlic 10 minutes into cooking time and rosemary in the last 5 minutes.

5 Season smashed potatoes generously with sea salt. Serve with roast garlic and rosemary sprigs.

**prep + cook time
55 minutes serves 6**

SIDE SALADS

ITALIAN-STYLE RICE SALAD

Heat 2 x 8.8oz (500g) pouches of cooked brown rice according to package directions; transfer to a large bowl. Add ½ cup (75g) sun-dried tomato strips (not in oil), ⅓ cup (15g) basil leaves, 2 cups (60g) coarsely chopped baby spinach, ⅔ cup (80g) sliced pitted Sicilian green olives, 1 thinly sliced small red onion, and ¼ cup (60ml) balsamic dressing. Season to taste. Toss gently to combine.

EDAMAME SLAW

Place 2 cups (160g) finely shredded red cabbage, 2 cups (150g) shredded carrot, ½ cup (70g) unsalted roasted peanuts, 1 finely chopped long red chili pepper, 1½ cups (400g) peeled and blanched edamame, and ½ cup (125ml) Asian-style sesame, soy and ginger dressing in a large bowl. Season to taste. Toss gently to combine.

prep time 15 minutes
(+ cooling)
serves 4

LENTIL TABBOULEH

Place 2 x 14oz (400g) cans drained lentils, 1 cup (20g) each of small flat-leaf parsley and mint leaves, 4 sliced scallions, 4oz (250g) sliced heirloom cherry tomatoes, ¼ cup (60ml) lemon juice, and ¼ cup (60ml) olive oil in a large bowl. Season to taste. Toss gently to combine.

KALE, PEAR, SMOKED CHEDDAR & ALMOND SALAD

Place 2 cups (60g) chopped kale, 1 medium cored and thinly sliced pear, ⅓ cup (40g) finely grated smoked Cheddar cheese, ¼ cup (40g) chopped roasted almonds, 2 tbsp lemon juice, and 1 tbsp olive oil in a large bowl. Season to taste. Toss gently to combine.

4 WAYS

ITALIAN-STYLE
RICE SALAD

LENTIL
TABBOULEH

EDAMAME
SLAW

KALE, PEAR,
SMOKED
CHEDDAR &
ALMOND SALAD

BRUSSELS SPROUTS REVOLUTION

10oz (300g) broccoli
10oz (300g) small Brussels sprouts
8oz (240g) kale, stems removed
   and discarded
2 tbsp extra-virgin olive oil
2 tbsp honey
salt and pepper to taste
oil for misting
2 garlic cloves, thinly sliced
2½oz (75g) prosciutto
⅓ cup (80g) chopped
   roasted almonds

GREEN TAHINI
2 tbsp tahini
2 tbsp lemon juice
2 tbsp cold water
1 tbsp extra-virgin olive oil
⅓ cup (15g) baby spinach leaves

1 Preheat a 5.3-quart air fryer to 400°F/200°C for 3 minutes.

2 Cut broccoli into florets. Trim base and remove tough outer leaves from Brussels sprouts. Tear leaves from kale into smaller pieces.

3 Combine olive oil and honey in a medium bowl. Add broccoli and Brussels sprouts; toss to coat. Season to taste.

4 Carefully place broccoli mixture in the air-fryer basket; cook for 8 minutes, stirring halfway through cooking time, or until vegetables are beginning to crisp at edges.

5 Place kale leaves in the basket and spray with oil; cook for 4 minutes.

6 Place garlic and prosciutto on top of vegetables; cook for 5 minutes, until prosciutto is crisp.

7 Meanwhile, to make green tahini, blend or process ingredients until smooth; season to taste. Add a little more water, if needed, to achieve a drizzling consistency.

8 Serve veggie mixture with crumbled prosciutto, drizzled with green tahini, and topped with almonds.

**prep + cook time
35 minutes serves 4**

GOLDEN ONION RINGS

¼ cup (35g) all-purpose flour
1 tsp smoked paprika
salt and pepper to taste
1 egg
1 tbsp cold water
1½ cups (110g) panko bread crumbs
2 medium onions, cut into ½in (1cm)
    slices, separated into rings
olive oil for misting
to serve: aïoli

1 Combine flour and paprika in a shallow bowl; season with salt and freshly ground black pepper. Lightly beat egg and the cold water in a second shallow bowl. Place bread crumbs in a third shallow bowl. Dust onion rings in flour mixture, shaking off excess, dip in egg, then coat in bread crumbs; spray generously all over with olive oil.
2 Preheat a 7-quart air fryer to 375°F/190°C for 3 minutes.
3 Carefully place half of the onion rings in the air-fryer basket; cook for 5 minutes or until golden and tender. Transfer to a wire rack. Repeat cooking with remaining onion rings.
4 Serve onion rings with aïoli.

**prep + cook time
25 minutes serves 4**

VEGGIE MAC 'N' CHEESE CROQUETTES

You will need to start this recipe
    a day ahead.
1⅓ cups (240g) macaroni
1 medium zucchini, finely chopped
1 cup (140g) frozen peas and corn
4 tbsp (60g) butter
1⅓ cups (200g) all-purpose flour
2 cups (500ml) milk
1 tsp Dijon mustard
2 scallions, thinly sliced
1 small red bell pepper,
    finely chopped
½ cup (60g) grated mozzarella
    cheese
¼ cup (30g) grated Cheddar cheese
¼ cup (20g) grated Parmesan
    cheese
2 eggs
2 cups (150g) panko bread crumbs
¼ cup finely chopped chives
olive oil for misting
to serve: sea salt flakes and
    tomato chutney

1 Grease an 8in x 12in (20cm x 30cm) pan; line bottom and sides with parchment paper, extending parchment 2in (5cm) over edges.
2 Cook pasta in a large saucepan of boiling salted water according to the package directions, adding zucchini and frozen peas and corn for the last 3 minutes of cooking time; drain well. Return pasta and vegetables to pan.
3 Meanwhile, make cheese sauce. Melt butter in a medium saucepan over medium-high heat. Add ⅓ cup (50g) of the flour; cook, stirring, for 2 minutes or until bubbling. Gradually stir in milk; cook, stirring, for 5 minutes or until sauce boils and thickens. Remove from heat; stir in mustard, scallions, red bell pepper, and cheeses until cheese is melted.
4 Pour cheese sauce over pasta and vegetables in saucepan; stir to combine. Spoon pasta mixture into lined pan; smooth the surface. Refrigerate for 6 hours or overnight.
5 Turn firm pasta mixture onto a clean work surface; cut into 1½in (4cm) pieces. Put remaining flour in a shallow bowl. Lightly whisk eggs in a second shallow bowl. Mix bread crumbs and chives in a third shallow bowl. Dust pasta pieces in flour, shaking off excess, dip in egg, then coat in bread crumb mixture; place on a sheet pan. Refrigerate for 15 minutes.
6 Preheat a 7-quart air fryer to 400°F/200°C for 3 minutes.
7 Spray croquettes generously all over with olive oil. Carefully place half of the croquettes in the air-fryer basket in a single layer; cook for 10 minutes, turning halfway through cooking time, or until crisp and golden. Using a spatula or slotted turner, carefully transfer to a plate; cover loosely with foil to keep warm. Repeat cooking with remaining croquettes.
8 Sprinkle croquettes with sea salt flakes and serve with tomato chutney.

**prep + cook time
50 minutes
(+ refrigeration)
serves 4**

ROASTED SQUASH
WITH PEPITA SALSA

2lb (1kg) kabocha squash, unpeeled, cut into 1¼in (3cm) thick wedges
2 tbsp extra-virgin olive oil
salt and pepper to taste
¼ cup (50g) pepitas, toasted
8oz (225g) feta, crumbled
to serve: flat-leaf parsley leaves

PEPITA SALSA
½ cup (100g) pepitas, toasted
1 cup (20g) flat-leaf parsley leaves
½ cup (125ml) extra-virgin olive oil
⅓ cup (80ml) lime juice
1 small garlic clove, crushed

1 Preheat a 5.3-quart air fryer to 400°F/200°C for 3 minutes.
2 Place squash wedges and oil in a large bowl; season with salt and freshly ground black pepper. Using your fingers, massage the oil onto each squash wedge.
3 Carefully place squash upright in the air-fryer basket; cook for 40 minutes, turning a number of times during cooking time, until tender.
4 Meanwhile, to make pepita salsa, blend or process ingredients until mixture forms a slightly chunky salsa; season to taste.

5 Serve squash wedges topped with pepita salsa, toasted pumpkin seeds, feta, and parsley leaves.

PREP IT Pepita salsa can be made up to 4 days ahead; refrigerate in a screw-top jar, covered with a thin layer of extra-virgin olive oil, until needed.

**prep + cook time 1 hour
serves 6**

POTATO GRATIN

1½lb (750g) russet potatoes, peeled
⅔ cup (160ml) light cream, warmed
⅓ cup (80ml) milk, warmed
2 garlic cloves, crushed
1 tbsp rosemary leaves
salt and pepper to taste
1 small onion, thinly sliced
1 cup (120g) grated Gruyère cheese
to serve: sea salt flakes

1 Using a mandolin, V-slicer, or sharp knife, slice potatoes very thinly.
2 Whisk cream, milk, garlic, and rosemary in a large bowl until combined; season with salt and freshly ground black pepper.
3 Layer potato slices, onion, and cream mixture in an 8in (20cm) round ovenproof dish, finishing with the cream mixture. Using your hands, press down firmly on the potatoes.
4 Preheat a 7-quart air fryer to 325°F/160°C for 3 minutes.

5 Carefully place the dish in the air-fryer basket; cook for 25 minutes, until potatoes are just tender.
6 Sprinkle the Gruyère cheese on top of the potatoes; cook for a further 5 minutes, or until cheese is golden.
7 Sprinkle with sea salt flakes to serve.

prep + cook time
45 minutes serves 6

LOADED CORN

6 ears of corn, in husks
3½oz (100g) fresh goat cheese, crumbled
finely grated zest of 1 lime
¼ cup (7g) cilantro leaves
¼ cup (20g) fried shallots
to serve: lime wedges

SRIRACHA & LIME BUTTER
½ cup (125g) butter, chopped, softened
¼ cup (70g) sriracha chili sauce
2 tsp lime juice

1 Cook corn in their husks in a large saucepan of boiling salted water for 3 minutes or until almost tender; drain and let cool. Peel back husks; remove and discard silks. Tie the husks back with kitchen twine.
2 Preheat a 5.3-quart air fryer to 400°F/200°C for 3 minutes.
3 Bend husks back so that corn will fit in the air-fryer basket; wrap just the husks of each ear in foil to prevent burning.
4 Carefully place half of the corn in the air-fryer basket; cook for 10 minutes. Transfer to a plate; cover to keep warm. Repeat cooking with remaining corn.
5 Meanwhile, to make sriracha and lime butter, process butter in a small food processor until whipped. Add sriracha and lime juice; process until smooth.
6 Spread sriracha and lime butter on hot corn; top with goat cheese, lime zest, cilantro, and fried shallots. Serve with lime wedges.

**prep + cook time
35 minutes makes 6**

ASPARAGUS WITH PROSCIUTTO
& GARLIC BUTTER

24 asparagus spears, trimmed
4 slices of prosciutto,
  halved lengthwise
olive oil for misting
2 tbsp (30g) butter
1 garlic clove, crushed
2 tsp thyme leaves
salt and pepper to taste

1 Preheat a 7-quart air fryer to 350°F/180°C for 3 minutes.

2 Group asparagus into bundles of three spears each. Wrap a slice of prosciutto around each bundle to secure; spray all over with olive oil.

3 Carefully place asparagus bundles in the air-fryer basket; cook for 6 minutes, turning halfway through cooking time, until prosciutto is golden and asparagus is tender.

4 Meanwhile, to make garlic butter, cook butter and garlic in a small skillet over medium heat until butter is melted; stir in thyme. Season with salt and freshly ground black pepper.

5 Serve asparagus bundles drizzled with garlic butter.

**prep + cook time
15 minutes serves 4**

HASSELBACK SWEET POTATOES

6 small sweet potatoes
4 tbsp (60g) butter, melted
2 garlic cloves, crushed
½ tsp ground cinnamon
2 tsp sea salt flakes
3½oz (100g) sliced round pancetta
    (use smoked pancetta slices if
    can't find rolled pancetta)
1 tbsp chopped chives

WHIPPED CHIVE BUTTER
6 tbsp (80g) butter, softened
1 tsp maple syrup
2 tbsp chopped chives

1 Wash unpeeled sweet potatoes; place on a cutting board. Trim a little piece lengthwise from one side so that they sit flat. Place a chopstick on the board along each side of a sweet potato. Slice crosswise at ½in (1cm) intervals, cutting through to the chopsticks (the chopsticks will prevent you from cutting all the way through). Repeat with remaining sweet potatoes.
2 Preheat a 5.3-quart air fryer to 400°F/200°C for 3 minutes.
3 Combine butter, garlic, cinnamon, and sea salt flakes in a small bowl. Brush butter mixture over sweet potatoes.
4 Carefully place sweet potatoes in the air-fryer basket; cook for 15 minutes.
5 Place pancetta on top of sweet potatoes; cook for a further 5 minutes until sweet potatoes are tender when pierced with the tip of a knife and the pancetta is crisp.
6 Meanwhile, to make whipped chive butter, beat butter in a small bowl with an electric mixer until light and fluffy. Beat in maple syrup, then stir in chives.
7 Spread sweet potatoes with whipped chive butter. Serve topped with crisp pancetta and sprinkled with chopped chives.

SWAP IT You can use any type of sweet potato or even regular potatoes. If using regular potatoes, omit the cinnamon and use paprika instead. Regular potatoes will discolor when cut, so prepare close to serving.

**prep + cook time 1 hour
serves 6**

PREP IT Sweet potatoes can be prepared to the end of step 3 up to 6 hours ahead; refrigerate until needed. Preheat the air fryer just before you're ready to cook.

SPICY CAJUN
POTATO WEDGES

PAPRIKA POTATO
WEDGES

SWEET
POTATO
WEDGES

LEMON PEPPER FRIES

CHILI GARLIC FRIES

SALTED FRIES

SPICY CAJUN POTATO WEDGES

Preheat a 5.3-quart air fryer to 400°F/200°C for 3 minutes. Cut 2lb (1kg) unpeeled fingerling potatoes into wedges. Combine 2 tbsp olive oil, 2 tsp ground cumin, 1 tsp ground coriander, 1 tsp hot paprika, ½ tsp ground oregano, ½ tsp ground black pepper, and ¼ tsp chili powder in a large bowl. Add wedges and toss to coat. Place wedges in the air-fryer basket; cook for 15–20 minutes, turning once, until golden and cooked. Season with salt and serve topped with oregano leaves.

PAPRIKA POTATO WEDGES

Preheat a 5.3-quart air fryer to 400°F/200°C for 3 minutes. Cut 2lb (1kg) russet potatoes into wedges. Place in a large bowl with 2 tbsp extra-virgin olive oil, 3 tbsp (40g) melted butter, and 2 tsp smoked paprika. Season with salt and toss to coat. Place wedges in the air-fryer basket; cook for 15–20 minutes, turning once, until golden and cooked. Sprinkle with ½ cup (40g) finely grated Parmesan cheese and serve with garlic mayonnaise.

6 WAYS HAND-CUT FRIES & WEDGES

SWEET POTATO WEDGES WITH CHILI LIME SALT

Preheat a 5.3-quart air fryer to 400°F/200°C for 3 minutes. Cut 2lb (1kg) sweet potatoes into wedges. Toss with 2 tbsp olive oil. Place wedges in the air-fryer basket; cook for 15–20 minutes, turning once, or until golden and cooked. Combine 2 tsp finely grated lime zest, 2 tbsp sea salt flakes, and 1 tsp chili flakes in a small heatproof bowl; place in air fryer for the last 3 minutes of cooking time to dry out the zest. Sprinkle wedges with chili lime salt to serve.

SALTED FRIES

Cut 2lb (1kg) peeled russet potatoes lengthwise into ½in (1cm) thick slices, then cut slices lengthwise into ½in (1cm) thick batons. Place in a large bowl of cold water. Let stand for 30 minutes; drain, then pat dry with paper towels. Toss with 2 tbsp olive oil. Preheat a 5.3-quart air fryer to 400°F/200°C for 3 minutes. Place fries in the air-fryer basket; cook for 15–20 minutes, turning once, until golden and cooked. Season with salt.

LEMON PEPPER FRIES

Make a batch of Salted Fries (below left), omitting the salt. Combine 1 tbsp finely grated lemon zest, ½ tsp freshly ground black pepper, and 1 tsp sea salt flakes in a small bowl. Sprinkle hot fries with lemon pepper and serve with lemon wedges.

swap it Use grated lime zest instead of lemon zest and crushed Sichuan peppercorns instead of black pepper.

serving suggestion These fries go well with battered or grilled fish, or with fish sandwiches, shrimp, and chicken.

CHILI GARLIC FRIES

Make a batch of Salted Fries (left). Heat 2 tsp olive oil in a small skillet. Cook 2 sliced long red chilies until soft. Add 2 sliced garlic cloves; cook, stirring, until fragrant. Sprinkle hot fries with chili mixture to serve.

serving suggestion These fries go well with hamburgers, grilled or pan-fried steak, and lamb cutlets.

BEETS
WITH YOGURT & DUKKAH

1½lb (700g) mixed baby beets, scrubbed, unpeeled (see tip)
2 tbsp extra-virgin olive oil
salt and pepper to taste
1½ tbsp dukkah spice mix
½ cup (140g) Greek-style yogurt
1 tbsp lemon juice
to serve: extra-virgin olive oil and flat-leaf parsley leaves

1 Preheat a 7-quart air fryer to 350°F/180°C for 3 minutes.
2 Quarter, halve, or cut beets into wedges so that all the pieces are a similar size. Place beets and oil in a large bowl; season with salt and pepper. Using your fingers, massage the oil into each beet wedge (wear gloves if you don't want to stain your hands).
3 Carefully place beets, cut-side up, in the air-fryer basket; cook for 25 minutes, turning a number of times, until tender. Sprinkle dukkah over beets for the last 5 minutes of cooking time.

4 Meanwhile, combine yogurt and lemon juice in a small bowl; season to taste.
5 To serve, spread yogurt mixture on a serving plate or platter; top with dukkah-spiced beets. Drizzle with extra olive oil and sprinkle with flat-leaf parsley leaves. Sprinkle with any dukkah that may have fallen through the basket holes into the pan.

**prep + cook time
35 minutes serves 4**

TIP You can also use
regular beets, cut into
¾in (1.5cm) wedges.

EPIC BAKED POTATOES

---

8 russet potatoes
extra-virgin olive oil for misting
½ tsp sea salt flakes
to serve: butter

1 Preheat a 5.3-quart air fryer to 400°F/200°C for 3 minutes.

2 Prick potatoes all over with a fork. Carefully place potatoes in the air-fryer basket, then spray with olive oil, and sprinkle with salt flakes; cook for 40 minutes, turning halfway through cooking time, until tender when pierced with the tip of a knife.

3 Transfer potatoes to plates. Cut a cross in the top of each potato, then squeeze upward from the bottom to open up. Serve with lashings of butter or with one of the toppers.

TOPPERS

nachos Heat a 1 x 15oz (440g) can pinto or ranch beans in a small saucepan. Top baked potatoes with ½ cup (25g) tortilla chips, then the beans; top with 1 cup (120g) grated Cheddar cheese. Return topped potatoes to the air-fryer basket; cook an additional 2 minutes, until cheese melts. To serve, top with ½ cup (120g) sour cream, 1 fresh sliced jalapeño, and ¼ cup (7g) cilantro leaves. Drizzle with your favorite chili sauce. Season to taste.

baked barbecue beans
Place 8oz (250g) halved cherry tomatoes in a medium saucepan with 1 x 15oz (425g) can baked beans, 1 tablespoon Dijon mustard, and 1 tablespoon smoky barbecue sauce; cook over medium heat, stirring occasionally, until mixture is heated through. To serve, top baked potatoes with baked bean mixture and ¼ cup (20g) finely grated Parmesan cheese. Season to taste.

TIP To reduce the air-fryer time, par-cook the potatoes first. Prick them all over with a fork, then microwave on HIGH (100%) for 8 minutes or until soft. Bake in the air fryer for 15 minutes.

prep + cook time
45 minutes serves 4

SESAME & CHILI BROCCOLINI
WITH MUSHROOMS

2 bunches of broccolini, trimmed
2 long red chilies, seeded,
    thickly sliced
6½oz (200g) mixed mushrooms,
    sliced (see tip)
1 tbsp sesame oil
salt and pepper to taste
3 garlic cloves, thinly sliced
1 tbsp sesame seeds
2 tbsp oyster sauce

1 Preheat a 7-quart air fryer to 350°F/180°C for 3 minutes.
2 Combine broccolini, chilies, and mushrooms in a large bowl, then add sesame oil; toss to coat. Season with salt and freshly ground black pepper.
3 Carefully place vegetable mixture in the air-fryer basket; cook for 10 minutes, tossing halfway through cooking time, or until vegetables are beginning to crisp at edges.
4 Sprinkle vegetables with garlic and sesame seeds; cook for a further 3 minutes until tender.
5 Serve vegetables drizzled with oyster sauce.

TIP We used shiitake, king oyster, oyster, and button mushrooms.

prep + cook time
25 minutes serves 4

CARROT RÖSTI

WITH PARMESAN & THYME

2 medium carrots, coarsely grated
1 medium russet potato,
   coarsely grated
½ small onion, coarsely grated
2 eggs, lightly beaten
½ cup (25g) finely grated Parmesan
   cheese
1 tbsp cornstarch
1 tbsp finely chopped thyme leaves
1 garlic clove, crushed
salt and pepper to taste
olive oil for misting
to serve: sea salt flakes and
   sour cream

1 Preheat a 7-quart air fryer to 400°F/200°C for 3 minutes.
2 Combine carrot, potato, onion, eggs, Parmesan cheese, cornstarch, thyme, and garlic in a large bowl, then season; mix well. Shape carrot mixture into eight ½in (1cm) thick round rösti, pressing each firmly between hands to compact; spray all over with olive oil.
3 Spray the air-fryer basket with olive oil. Carefully, place rösti in the basket; cook for 14 minutes, turning halfway through cooking time, until golden and tender.
4 Sprinkle rösti with sea salt flakes and serve with sour cream.

**prep + cook time
35 minutes serves 4
(makes 8)**

CRISP TOFU
WITH PALM SUGAR DRESSING

1lb (600g) medium tofu
2 bunches of broccolini, trimmed,
    thick stems halved lengthwise
5½oz (170g) swiss chard, trimmed,
    cut into 2in (5cm) lengths
3 egg whites
1 cup (180g) rice flour
2 tbsp sesame seeds
1 tbsp ground white pepper
2 tsp freshly ground black pepper
2 tsp salt
olive oil for misting
to serve: sliced scallions, sliced red
    chili, extra sesame seeds, and
    lime wedges

PALM SUGAR DRESSING
1 tbsp finely grated fresh ginger
¼ cup (60ml) extra-virgin olive oil
2 tbsp lime juice
¼ cup (60ml) mirin
¼ cup (60ml) soy sauce
1 tbsp palm sugar
1 small red chili, finely chopped

1 Cut tofu horizontally into four slices; cut each slice in half to make eight pieces in total. Line a cutting board with paper towels. Place tofu slices on paper towels; lay more paper towels on top of tofu, then top with a heavy pan (or small cutting board) to weigh down the tofu. Leave for 10 minutes to drain.

2 Preheat a 5.3-quart air fryer to 350°F/180°C for 3 minutes.

3 Rinse broccolini and Swiss chard. Carefully place damp vegetables in the air-fryer basket; cook for 5 minutes until just tender. Transfer to a platter; cover to keep warm.

4 Meanwhile, to make palm sugar dressing, place ingredients in a screw-top jar; shake well to combine.

5 Beat egg whites in a shallow bowl. Combine rice flour, sesame seeds, white and black peppers, and salt in a second shallow bowl. Dip tofu slices in egg white, then coat in rice flour mixture; spray generously with oil.

6 Place half of the tofu in the basket; cook for 15 minutes, turning halfway through cooking time, or until crisp and golden. Transfer to a wire rack. Repeat cooking with remaining tofu.

7 Top vegetables with crisp tofu, sliced scallions, sliced chili, and extra sesame seeds; drizzle with dressing. Serve with lime wedges.

prep + cook time
45 minutes
serves 4

WEEKENDS

The air fryer might be the best appliance for fast and easy cooking during the week, but it's also a superstar when it comes to cooking larger cuts of meat and fish, as well as more ambitious recipes.

STEAK
WITH BÉARNAISE & FRIES

1½lb (600g) russet potatoes, cut into
    ½in (1cm) fries
olive oil for misting
4 x 6oz (185g) rib-eye steaks, cut
    ¾in (2cm) thick
salt and pepper to taste
2 cups (240g) frozen peas

BÉARNAISE SAUCE
½ cup (125ml) dry white wine
2 tbsp white wine vinegar
2 shallots, finely chopped
1 tsp dried tarragon
1 tsp black peppercorns
3 egg yolks
1 cup (250g) butter, melted
1 tbsp finely chopped fresh tarragon

1 To make Béarnaise sauce, combine wine, vinegar, shallots, dried tarragon, and peppercorns in a small saucepan; simmer for 5 minutes or until liquid reduces to about 2 tablespoons. Strain through a fine sieve into a heatproof bowl; discard the shallot mixture. Place bowl containing wine mixture over a saucepan of simmering water (make sure the bowl doesn't touch the water). Add egg yolks to the bowl; whisk for 3 minutes, or until the mixture is pale and frothy. Add butter, 1 tablespoon at a time, whisking continuously after each addition until sauce is thick and smooth. Remove from heat. Stir in fresh tarragon; season. Cover pan and set aside until needed.

2 Preheat an 11-quart air fryer to 400°F/200°C for 3 minutes.

3 Spray fries all over with olive oil; spread out on two of the air-fryer racks.

4 Carefully slide the racks onto the lower shelves of the air fryer; cook for 20 minutes, rotating racks halfway through cooking time.

5 Place steaks on the remaining rack. Spray both sides with oil and season. Carefully slide the rack into the second-highest shelf of the air fryer; cook for 7 minutes, turning after 2 minutes, or until steaks are medium or cooked to your liking and fries are golden and tender. Transfer steaks to a plate; cover loosely with foil and let rest for 5 minutes.

6 Meanwhile, boil, steam or microwave peas until just tender; drain.

7 Season steaks with freshly ground black pepper. Serve with Béarnaise sauce, fries, and peas.

prep + cook time 1 hour serves 4

TIPS Do not position the steaks on the highest shelf in the air fryer, as this can cause the appliance to smoke. For a smaller 7-quart air fryer, cook the fries first, then transfer to a plate while you cook the steaks. While the steaks are resting, reheat the fries in the air fryer.

MINI MEATLOAVES

WRAPPED IN MAPLE BACON

½ small onion, finely grated

⅓ cup (10g) finely chopped
   flat-leaf parsley

2 garlic cloves, crushed

½ cup (50g) packaged bread crumbs

1 egg, lightly beaten

¼ cup (70g) ketchup

1 tbsp Worcestershire sauce

1lb (450g) ground beef

salt and pepper to taste

1 tbsp chopped thyme leaves

4 slices thick-cut bacon

½ tbsp maple syrup

to serve: extra ketchup

1 Preheat a 7-quart air fryer to 350°F/180°C for 3 minutes.

2 Combine onion, parsley, garlic, bread crumbs, egg, ketchup, Worcestershire sauce, and beef in a large bowl, then season with salt and freshly ground black pepper; mix well to combine. Divide mixture into four even portions and shape each into a small loaf. Sprinkle with thyme, then wrap in bacon.

3 Carefully place meatloaves, top-side down, in the air-fryer basket; cook for 20 minutes, turning halfway through cooking time. Brush tops with maple syrup during the last 5 minutes of cooking time.

4 Serve meatloaves with extra ketchup.

SERVE IT Wrap meatloaves in romaine or iceberg lettuce leaves for a crunchy finish.

**prep + cook time
40 minutes serves 4**

MATCH IT Peri-Peri Potatoes, page 145.

SPICY KOREAN PEANUT PORK RIBS

4½lb (2kg) pork ribs
2 garlic cloves, crushed
1 tsp finely grated fresh ginger
¼ cup (95g) crunchy peanut butter
1 tbsp sriracha chili sauce
1 tbsp soy sauce
2 tsp fish sauce
1 tbsp light soft brown sugar
2 tsp sesame oil
2 tbsp lime juice
½ cup (125ml) coconut cream
oil for misting
2 cucumbers, seeded, halved
    lengthwise, thinly sliced
2 long red chilies, finely chopped
salt and pepper to taste
2 tbsp water
to serve: lime wedges and
    steamed jasmine rice

1 Using a small, sharp knife, remove the layer of membrane from the back of the ribs (or ask your butcher to do this for you). Place ribs in a large saucepan and cover well with water; bring to a boil over medium heat. Reduce heat; simmer for 45 minutes or until almost tender.

2 Meanwhile, to make marinade, blend or process garlic, ginger, peanut butter, sauces, sugar, sesame oil, and half of the lime juice until smooth. Add coconut cream; blend until combined. Transfer to a large nonmetallic dish. Drain ribs; add to marinade and turn to coat. Cover. Refrigerate for 2 hours.

3 Preheat a 7-quart air fryer to 350°F/180°C for 3 minutes.

4 Spray the air-fryer basket with oil. Remove ribs from the marinade, scraping off any that has solidified; reserve remaining marinade. Carefully arrange the ribs in the basket, standing them up and leaning them against the side of the basket and one another. Reset the temperature to 325°F/160°C; cook for 20 minutes.

5 Brush ribs with a third of the reserved marinade; cook for a further 10 minutes until tender and glazed.

6 Meanwhile, combine cucumber, chilies, and remaining lime juice in a small bowl; season. Let stand for 10 minutes.

7 To make peanut sauce, place remaining reserved marinade and 2 tablespoons water in a small saucepan over medium-high heat; bring to a boil. Reduce heat; simmer for 4 minutes or until thickened slightly.

8 Cut ribs into serving-sized pieces and place on a large platter; spoon over a little peanut sauce. Serve with remaining peanut sauce, the cucumber mixture, lime wedges, and jasmine rice.

prep + cook time
1 hour 40 minutes
(+ refrigeration)
serves 4

CHICKEN & LEEK PIE

2 cups (500ml) chicken stock
1¼lb (625g) boneless skinless
   chicken breasts
2 sheets of frozen butter puff
   pastry, just thawed
1 egg, lightly beaten
oil for misting
4 tbsp (60g) butter
1 large leek, thinly sliced
2 stalks celery, trimmed,
   finely chopped
2 tbsp all-purpose flour
2 tsp thyme leaves
½ cup (125ml) milk
1 cup (250ml) light cream
2 tsp whole grain mustard

1 Bring stock to a boil in a medium saucepan. Add chicken; return to a boil. Reduce heat; simmer, covered, for 10 minutes or until chicken is cooked through. Remove from heat. Allow chicken to stand in poaching liquid for 10 minutes.
2 Preheat a 5.3-quart air fryer to 350°F/180°C for 3 minutes.
3 Stack pastry sheets on top of one another. Place a 6in x 8¾in (15cm x 22cm), 1.5-quart rectangular dish over pastry stack; cut around it to cut out a rectangle the same size, then cut four slits crosswise in the center of the pastry. (Alternatively, use another-sized dish, but no larger than the pastry sheet.)
4 Brush pastry with egg. Spray the air-fryer basket with oil. Carefully place pastry stack in the basket;

cook for 15–18 minutes until pastry is puffed and deep golden.
5 Meanwhile, remove chicken from liquid; coarsely chop. Reserve 1 cup (250ml) of the poaching liquid. (Keep remaining liquid for another use or discard.) Heat butter in a medium saucepan; cook leek and celery, stirring, until leek softens. Add flour and thyme; cook, stirring, for 1 minute. Gradually stir in reserved poaching liquid, the milk and cream; cook, stirring, until mixture boils and thickens. Stir in chopped chicken and the mustard. Season to taste.
6 Spoon hot chicken mixture into dish; carefully place cooked puff pastry on top. Serve pie sprinkled with extra thyme, if you like.

**prep + cook time
45 minutes serves 6**

PREP IT Pie filling can be made a day ahead; refrigerate until needed.

BUTTERFLIED HARISSA CHICKEN
WITH COUSCOUS & ORANGE

1 whole chicken, about 2½lb (1.4kg)
2 garlic cloves, crushed
2 tbsp lemon juice
2 tsp sweet paprika
1 tbsp harissa paste (see tip)
2 tbsp extra-virgin olive oil
olive oil for misting
1 cup (200g) couscous
1 cup (250ml) boiling water
½ cup (15g) cilantro leaves
salt and pepper to taste
2 medium oranges, peeled,
   thinly sliced
to serve: Greek-style yogurt and
   sea salt flakes

1 Place chicken, breast-side down, on a cutting board. Using poultry shears, cut down both sides of the backbone and discard. Open out the chicken, turn it over, and press down on the breastbone with the heel of your hand to flatten.

2 Combine garlic, lemon juice, paprika, harissa, and oil in a large shallow dish; add chicken and turn to coat. Cover dish. Refrigerate for at least 2 hours or overnight.

3 Preheat a 7-quart air fryer to 350°F/180°C for 5 minutes.

4 Spray the air-fryer basket with oil. Carefully place chicken, skin-side up, in the basket, then cover loosely with foil; cook for 20 minutes.

5 Remove foil; cook chicken for a further 20 minutes, until juices run clear when a skewer is inserted into the thickest part of a thigh. Transfer to a large dish; cover with foil and let rest for 10 minutes.

6 Meanwhile, combine couscous and the boiling water in a large heatproof bowl; cover and let stand for 5 minutes or until liquid is absorbed. Fluff couscous with a fork. Stir in cilantro and season to taste.

7 Serve chicken with couscous, oranges, and yogurt, drizzled with any cooking juices from the bottom of the air-fryer pan. Sprinkle with sea salt flakes.

TIP Harissa brands can vary in heat, so use according to taste.

prep + cook time 1 hour (+ refrigeration & standing) serves 4

TESTING MEAT

Insert a meat thermometer into the thickest part of the beef. The internal temperature should reach:

rare 130–140°F/ 55–60°C

medium-rare 140–150°F/60–65°C

medium 150–160°F/65–70°C

medium–well done 160–170°F/70–75°C

well-done 170°F/75°C

HERB-CRUSTED ROAST BEEF

WITH CREAMY MUSHROOMS

2½lb (1.2kg) rib-eye roast
1 tbsp olive oil
salt and pepper to taste
⅔ cup (80g) panko bread crumbs
¼ cup (20g) finely grated Parmesan cheese
2 tbsp chopped flat-leaf parsley
1 tbsp chopped tarragon
¼ cup chopped chives
3 garlic cloves, crushed
¼ cup (70g) whole grain mustard
1 tsp smoked paprika
olive oil for misting
5oz (150g) baby portabella mushrooms, halved (or quartered if large)
5oz (150g) button mushrooms, halved (or quartered if large)
¾ cup (180ml) heavy cream
to serve: roast potatoes

1 Preheat a 7-quart air fryer to 400°F/200°C for 5 minutes.

2 Brush beef with 2 teaspoons of the oil and season.

3 Carefully place beef in the air-fryer basket; cook for 15 minutes, turning halfway through cooking time, until browned all over.

4 Meanwhile, combine the bread crumbs, Parmesan cheese, parsley, tarragon, half of the chives, and half of the garlic in a bowl; season. Transfer beef to a plate and pat dry with paper towels. Working quickly, spread 2 tablespoons of the mustard over the top and sides of beef, sprinkle with paprika, then firmly press on bread crumb mixture. Generously spray bread crumbs with oil.

5 Return beef to the air-fryer basket. Cover basket tightly with foil. Reset the temperature to 350°F/180°C; cook for 30 minutes. Remove foil.

6 Toss mushrooms in remaining oil and add to the air-fryer basket; cook, without foil, for a further 10 minutes, until beef is medium or cooked to your liking (see Testing Meat to left) and mushrooms are browned. Transfer beef to a dish; cover loosely with foil and let rest for 15 minutes.

7 Meanwhile, to make creamy mushrooms, combine cream and remaining garlic and mustard in a medium saucepan over medium heat. Add the mushrooms and any cooking juices from the bottom of the air-fryer pan; bring to a boil. Reduce heat; simmer, stirring occasionally, for 5 minutes or until sauce slightly thickens. Stir in remaining chives and season to taste.

8 Thinly slice beef and serve with creamy mushrooms and roast potatoes.

MATCH IT Roast Potatoes 4 Ways, page 145.

prep + cook time 1 hour 20 minutes serves 6

TIKKA LAMB CHOPS
WITH CARROT KOSHIMBIR

⅓ cup (80g) tikka masala spice paste
1 tbsp lemon juice
½ cup (140g) Greek-style yogurt
12 French-trimmed lamb
   chops (600g)
olive oil for misting
to serve: steamed basmati rice
   and warm naan bread

CARROT KOSHIMBIR
2 medium carrots, coarsely grated
½ cup (25g) shredded coconut
¼ cup (10g) firmly packed cilantro
   leaves
1 long green chili, thinly sliced
2 tbsp lemon juice
salt and pepper to taste

1 Combine spice paste, lemon juice, and half of the yogurt in a large bowl; add lamb and toss to coat. Refrigerate for 1 hour.
2 Preheat a 7-quart air fryer to 400°F/200°C for 3 minutes.
3 To make carrot koshimbir, place carrots, coconut, half of the cilantro, the chili, and lemon juice in a bowl; mix well. Season.
4 Carefully line the air-fryer basket with a silicone mat, if available (see page 11). Spray lamb generously on both sides with oil and place in the basket; cook for 8 minutes, turning halfway through cooking time, for medium, or until cooked to your liking.

5 Meanwhile, finely chop remaining cilantro and stir into remaining yogurt.
6 Serve lamb chops with steamed rice, warm naan bread, carrot koshimbir, and cilantro yogurt.

**prep + cook time
20 minutes
(+ refrigeration)
serves 4**

GREEK-STYLE POTATOES

MUSTARD & MINT POTATOES

4 WAYS

PERI-PERI POTATOES

FETA, DILL & BACON POTATOES

GREEK-STYLE POTATOES

Preheat a 7-quart air fryer to 400°F/200°C for 3 minutes. Cut 2lb (1kg) baby potatoes into quarters lengthwise. Place in a large bowl with 2 tbsp olive oil, 2 tsp dried oregano, 2 tbsp finely chopped rosemary, and 4 crushed garlic cloves, then season; mix well to coat. Carefully place potatoes in the air-fryer basket; cook for 20 minutes, turning halfway through cooking time, until golden and tender. Serve drizzled with 2 tbsp lemon juice.

MUSTARD & MINT POTATOES

Preheat a 7-quart air fryer to 400°F/200°C for 3 minutes. Cut 2lb (1kg) unpeeled baby potatoes in half lengthwise. Place in a large bowl with 2 tbsp olive oil, then season; mix well to coat. Carefully place potatoes in the air-fryer basket; cook for 20 minutes, turning halfway through cooking time, until golden and tender. Meanwhile, combine 1 tsp each of Dijon mustard and whole grain mustard, 2 tbsp finely chopped mint, 1 tbsp olive oil, and 3 tsp white wine vinegar in a large bowl; add potatoes and toss to coat. Serve sprinkled with mint leaves.

ROAST POTATOES

prep + cook time 30 minutes serves 6

PERI-PERI POTATOES

Preheat a 7-quart air fryer to 400°F/200°C for 3 minutes. Cut 2lb (1kg) baby potatoes in half widthwise. Place in a large bowl with 2 tbsp olive oil, a ¾oz (25g) packet of medium peri-peri seasoning, and 3 crushed garlic cloves, then season; mix well to coat. Carefully place potatoes in the air-fryer basket; cook for 20 minutes, turning halfway through cooking time, until golden and tender. Drizzle with peri-peri sauce for extra heat, if you like.

FETA, DILL & BACON POTATOES

Preheat a 7-quart air fryer to 400°F/200°C for 3 minutes. Cut 2lb (1kg) baby potatoes into quarters. Place in a large bowl with 2 tbsp olive oil, then season; mix well to coat. Carefully place potatoes in the air-fryer basket; cook for 20 minutes, turning halfway through cooking time, until golden and tender. Add 4 slices thick-cut bacon to the air-fryer basket for the last 7 minutes of cooking time. Meanwhile, combine 2 tbsp (30g) crumbled feta, 1 tbsp chopped dill, 2 tbsp mayonnaise, and ¼ cup (65g) sour cream in a large bowl; add potatoes and toss to coat. Top with the crispy bacon and extra dill sprigs.

EGGPLANT PARMIGIANA "MEATBALL" SUBS

1 medium eggplant, peeled, cut into
  1½in (4cm) pieces
olive oil for misting
1 x 15oz (425g) can chickpeas,
  drained, rinsed
1 small red onion, finely chopped
2 garlic cloves, crushed
1 tbsp finely chopped
  rosemary leaves
1¾ cups (140g) finely grated
  Parmesan cheese
salt and pepper to taste
1½ cups (150g) packaged bread
  crumbs
6 long soft bread rolls
1 cup (260g) pasta sauce, heated
2 cups (40g) arugula leaves
2 tsp balsamic vinegar

1 Preheat a 5.3-quart air fryer to 400°F/200°C for 3 minutes. Line a sheet pan with parchment paper.

2 Carefully place the eggplant in the air-fryer basket and spray with oil; cook for 15 minutes, until golden and tender.

3 Transfer eggplant to a food processor with chickpeas, onion, garlic, rosemary, and 1 cup (80g) of the Parmesan cheese; process until combined. Season. Add 1 cup (100g) of the bread crumbs; pulse until combined. Roll level tablespoons of eggplant mixture into 24 balls, then coat in remaining bread crumbs; spray generously with olive oil.

4 Place eggplant balls in the basket; cook for 20 minutes, turning halfway through cooking time, or until golden and heated through.

5 Split rolls lengthwise along the top without cutting all the way through; spread sides with pasta sauce. Fill each roll with four eggplant "meatballs." Place rolls in the basket; cook for 5 minutes.

6 Meanwhile, combine arugula and vinegar in a small bowl.

7 To serve, sprinkle remaining Parmesan cheese over "meatball" subs and top with the arugula salad.

**prep + cook time 1 hour
serves 6**

LEMON & HERB PORK SCHNITZELS

½ cup (75g) all-purpose flour

2 eggs

⅓ cup (80ml) milk

2 garlic cloves, crushed

2 cups (150g) fresh bread crumbs

⅓ cup (25g) finely grated Parmesan cheese

¼ cup chopped chives

1 tbsp finely chopped lemon thyme

2 tsp finely grated lemon zest

1lb (450g) sliced pork tenderloin, pounded thinly

olive oil for misting

to serve: extra lemon thyme, sea salt flakes, aïoli, fries (see pages 116–117 or use frozen) and lemon wedges

1 Place flour in a shallow bowl. Lightly beat eggs, milk, and garlic in a second shallow bowl. Combine bread crumbs, Parmesan cheese, chives, thyme, and lemon zest in a third shallow bowl. Dust pork in flour, shaking off excess, dip in egg mixture, then coat in bread crumb mixture. Place schnitzels on a plate. Refrigerate for 30 minutes.

2 Preheat a 7-quart air fryer to 350°F/180°C for 3 minutes.

3 Spray schnitzels generously on both sides with olive oil. Carefully place half of the schnitzels in the air-fryer basket; cook for 10 minutes, turning halfway through cooking time, until golden and cooked through. Transfer to a plate; cover loosely with foil to keep warm. Repeat cooking with remaining schnitzels.

4 Sprinkle schnitzels with extra thyme and sea salt flakes. Serve with aïoli, fries, and lemon wedges.

**prep + cook time
40 minutes
(+ refrigeration)
serves 4**

MATCH IT Kale, Pear, Smoked Cheddar & Almond Salad, page 98.

RIDICULOUSLY
GOOD RIBS

5lb (2kg) pork ribs
olive oil for misting
1 cup (280g) barbecue sauce
3 cups (220g) shredded red cabbage
2 cups (180g) julienned carrot
1 medium green apple, unpeeled,
  cored and thinly sliced
½ cup (125ml) coleslaw dressing
2 scallions, green part only, very
  thinly sliced lengthwise (see tip)

MARINADE
⅓ cup (80ml) apple cider vinegar
2 tbsp Worcestershire sauce
2 tbsp honey
2 garlic cloves, crushed
1 tbsp extra-virgin olive oil

DRY SPICE RUB
1 tbsp smoked paprika
¼ tsp chili powder
1 tsp chili flakes
1½ tsp onion powder
1½ tsp garlic powder
2 tbsp light soft brown sugar

1 Using a small, sharp knife, remove the layer of membrane from the back of the ribs (or ask your butcher to do this for you). Place ribs in a large saucepan; cover well with water. Bring to a boil over medium heat. Reduce heat to a simmer; cook for 45 minutes or until ribs are almost tender.
2 Meanwhile, combine marinade ingredients in a large bowl and dry spice rub ingredients in a small bowl. Drain ribs; add to marinade and turn to coat. Remove from marinade and sprinkle with dry spice rub. Using your hands, rub spices all over ribs; spray with olive oil.
3 Preheat a 5.3-quart air fryer to 350°F/180°C for 3 minutes.
4 Carefully arrange ribs in the air-fryer basket, standing them up and leaning them against the side of the basket and one another. Reset the temperature to 325°F/160°C; cook for 20 minutes.
5 Brush ribs with three-quarters of the barbecue sauce; cook for 10 minutes until tender and glazed.
6 Meanwhile, combine cabbage, carrot, apple, and dressing in a medium bowl. Top with scallions.
7 Cut ribs into serving-sized pieces and brush with remaining barbecue sauce. Serve with coleslaw.

PREP IT You can prepare the ribs to the end of step 2 a day ahead; refrigerate until needed. As the ribs will be chilled, you may need to add an extra 5 minutes to the cooking time.
TIP To make scallion curls, put in a small bowl of iced water for 5–7 minutes. Drain before using.

prep + cook time
1½ hours serves 4

CORN & SWEET POTATO HASH BROWNS
WITH SAUSAGES

1½lb (750g) chopped sweet potato
oil for misting
2 ears of corn, husks removed
2 scallions, finely chopped
salt and pepper to taste
1lb (450g) breakfast sausage links
½ cup (90g) rice flour
2 eggs
1¾ cups (135g) shredded coconut
to serve: baby spinach leaves
    and tomato chutney

1 Place sweet potatoes in the basket of a 5.3-quart air fryer and spray with oil; at 350°F/180°C, cook for 20 minutes, turning halfway through cooking time.
2 Carefully add corn to the basket; cook for 5 minutes.
3 Transfer sweet potatoes to a bowl and mash. Using a sharp knife, cut kernels from corn cobs. Add kernels to mash with scallions, then season; mix well.
4 Place sausages in the basket; cook for 15 minutes, until browned and cooked through.
5 Meanwhile, shape heaped ⅓ cups of sweet potato mixture into patties; place on a sheet pan lined with parchment paper. Place rice flour in a bowl. Lightly beat eggs in a shallow bowl. Place shredded coconut in a third bowl. Dust patties in flour, shaking off excess, dip in egg, then coat in coconut. Return to lined sheet pan. Freeze for 10 minutes to set coating. (If not cooking immediately, refrigerate.)
6 Transfer sausages to a plate; cover to keep warm. Spray patties with oil on both sides and place in the basket. Reset the temperature to 325°F/160°C; cook for 10 minutes, turning halfway through cooking time, or until golden brown.
7 Serve sausages with hash browns, baby spinach leaves, and tomato chutney.

TIP If you would like to ensure this recipe is gluten-free, buy gluten-free sausages and tomato chutney.

prep + cook time
1¼ hours (+ refrigeration)
serves 4

CHEESY BACON PULL-APART

**prep + cook time 30 minutes
(+ standing) serves 8**

Divide 1 quantity Basic Dough (see recipe opposite)
into eight equal portions; roll each portion into
a ball. Arrange dough balls, ¾in (2cm) apart, in a
greased 9¼in (23cm) round cake pan; cover with
plastic wrap. Let stand in a warm place for
20 minutes or until doubled in size. Preheat a
7-quart air fryer to 400°F/200°C for 5 minutes.
Carefully place pan in the air-fryer basket.
Reset the temperature to 340°F/170°C; cook for
15 minutes. Brush bread with 2 tbsp (30g) melted
butter, then sprinkle with ¾ cup (50g) grated
Cheddar cheese and 4 slices of finely chopped
cooked bacon; cook for 8 minutes, until bread is
golden and cooked through.

GARLIC & PARMESAN TWIST

prep + cook time 40 minutes (+ standing) serves 6

Combine 1 tbsp olive oil, 2 tbsp (30g) melted butter,
3 crushed garlic cloves, and 2 tbsp finely chopped
chives. Divide 1 quantity Basic Dough (see recipe
opposite) into three portions; roll each portion into
a 12in (30cm) rope shape. Place ropes, side by side,
on a 10in (25cm) square piece of parchment paper;
pinch at one end to join. Brush with three-quarters
of the butter mixture, then sprinkle with 2 tbsp finely
grated Parmesan cheese. Braid ropes loosely, then
pinch end tightly to join; cover with a clean kitchen
towel. Let stand in a warm place for 20 minutes or
until doubled in size. Preheat a 7-quart air fryer to
400°F/200°C for 5 minutes. Using the parchment
paper as an aid, carefully lower the dough braid
diagonally into the air-fryer basket. Brush
with half of the remaining butter mixture. Reset
the temperature to 340°F/170°C; cook for 18
minutes. Brush with remaining butter mixture,
then sprinkle with 2 tbsp finely grated Parmesan
cheese; cook for 5 minutes until bread is golden and
cooked through.

TOMATO PESTO FOCACCIA

prep + cook time 40 minutes (+ standing) serves 6

Preheat a 7-quart air fryer to 400°F/200°C for
5 minutes. Roll 1 quantity Basic Dough (see recipe
opposite) into a 9¼in (23cm) round; place on a
large piece of parchment paper. Using fingertips,
press dimples all over the dough. Trim parchment
paper so that it is ¾in (2cm) larger all around than
the dough base. Using the parchment paper as an
aid, carefully lower the focaccia into the air-fryer
basket. Reset the temperature to 340°F/170°C;
cook for 15 minutes. Combine 1 tbsp olive oil and
2 tbsp sun-dried tomato pesto in a small bowl.
Spread pesto mixture over focaccia, then sprinkle
with 2 sliced garlic cloves and 1 tsp sea salt
flakes; cook for 7 minutes, until focaccia is
golden and cooked through. Top with basil
leaves to serve.

MIXED-SEED BUNS

prep + cook time 30 minutes (+ standing) serves 8

Combine ¼ cup pumpkin and sunflower seed mix,
2 tbsp pine nuts, 1 tbsp flax seeds, and 1 tbsp
sesame seeds. Knead half of the seed mixture into
1 quantity Basic Dough (see recipe opposite). Divide
dough into eight portions; roll each portion into a
ball. Place on a sheet pan lined with parchment
paper; cover with a clean kitchen towel. Let stand
in a warm place for 20 minutes or until doubled in
size. Preheat a 7-quart air fryer to 400°F/200°C for
5 minutes. Carefully line the air-fryer basket with
parchment paper. Place the dough balls ¾in (2cm)
apart in the basket. Cut three shallow slits on the
top of each dough ball. Lightly brush tops with 1
lightly beaten egg, then sprinkle with remaining
seed mixture. Reset the temperature to
340°F/170°C; cook for 15 minutes until buns are
golden and cooked through.

BASIC DOUGH

Combine 3 cups (390g) all-purpose flour, 2 tsp yeast, and 1 tsp salt in a large bowl. Add 1⅓ cups (330ml) lukewarm water; mix to form a dough. Knead dough on a lightly floured surface for 10 minutes (or 6 minutes in an electric mixer fitted with a dough hook) or until dough is smooth and elastic. Return dough to cleaned bowl; cover with plastic wrap. Let stand in a warm place for 30 minutes or until doubled in size. Using your fist, punch down dough to remove air. Knead on a lightly floured surface for 2 minutes or until smooth. Continue with one of the recipe variations to the left.

4 WAYS

BREAD

CHEESY BACON PULL-APART

TOMATO PESTO FOCACCIA

GARLIC & PARMESAN TWIST

MIXED-SEED BUNS

JAPANESE SALMON
WITH MISO SAUCE

---

2 tbsp mirin
2 tbsp cooking sake
2 tbsp soy sauce
1½lb (800g) center-cut fillet
   skinless boneless salmon
8 scallions, trimmed
2 tsp sesame seeds, toasted

MISO SAUCE
2 tbsp white (shiro) miso
2 tbsp rice wine vinegar
1½ tbsp honey
1½ tbsp soy sauce

1 To make yakitori marinade, combine mirin, sake, and soy sauce in a small bowl.
2 To make miso sauce, blend ingredients in a small blender until smooth.
3 Preheat a 5.3-quart air fryer to 325°F/160°C for 3 minutes.
4 Cut salmon into ¾in (2cm) pieces; thread onto six metal or bamboo skewers. Brush all over with the marinade.
5 Carefully line the air-fryer basket with parchment paper. Place scallions in the basket; acook for 5 minutes, until tender. Transfer to a platter; cover to keep warm.

6 Place half of the skewers in the basket; cook for 5 minutes or until cooked to your liking. Transfer to platter; cover to keep warm. Repeat cooking with remaining skewers.
7 Serve the salmon and scallions drizzled with miso sauce; sprinkle with sesame seeds.

SERVE IT Serve with microwaveable brown rice and quinoa, and lime wedges.

**prep + cook time
35 minutes makes 6**

SWAP IT The yakitori marinade and miso sauce also work well with large shrimp. If using shrimp, cook them for 5 minutes.

HOISIN PORK
WITH PEANUT RICE

⅓ cup (190g) hoisin sauce
⅓ cup (80ml) low-sodium soy sauce
2 tbsp Shaohsing rice wine
2 tbsp honey
¼ cup (55g) firmly packed
    light soft brown sugar
4 garlic cloves, crushed
½ tsp Chinese five-spice powder
4 x 4½oz (150g) pork
    shoulder steaks
2 x 8.8oz pouches (500g) of cooked
    jasmine rice
½ cup (70g) unsalted roasted
    peanuts, coarsely chopped
2 scallions, thinly sliced
4 baby cucumbers,
    thinly sliced lengthwise
to serve: extra hoisin sauce

1 Combine hoisin sauce, soy sauce, rice wine, honey, sugar, garlic, and five-spice powder in a large shallow dish; add pork and turn to coat. Cover dish. Refrigerate for at least 2 hours or overnight.
2 Line the bottom of a 7-quart air-fryer pan with foil. Preheat air fryer to 350°F/180°C for 3 minutes.
3 Carefully place pork in the air-fryer basket, reserving the marinade; at 350°F/180°C, cook for 15 minutes, turning and basting pork with reserved marinade halfway through cooking time.
4 Reset the temperature to 400°F/200°C; cook pork for a further 5 minutes,

basting with reserved marinade, or until charred and cooked through. Transfer to a dish; cover with foil and let rest for 5 minutes.
5 Meanwhile, heat rice according to package directions. Transfer to a medium heatproof bowl; stir in peanuts and half of the scallions.
6 Slice pork; serve with rice, cucumber, and remaining scallions. Drizzle pork with any cooking juices from the bottom of the air-fryer pan and extra hoisin sauce.

**prep + cook time
35 minutes
(+ refrigeration)
serves 4**

STUFFED LEG OF LAMB
WITH APRICOT & PISTACHIO

½ cup (80g) finely chopped
   dried apricots
¼ cup (60ml) orange juice
2 tbsp (30g) butter, chopped
1 medium onion, finely chopped
1 cup (100g) coarse fresh
   sourdough bread crumbs
¼ cup (30g) pistachios, roasted,
   finely chopped
2 tbsp finely chopped sage
2½lb (1.2kg) boneless leg of lamb
1 tbsp olive oil
1 garlic bulb, halved
1 cup (250ml) gravy, warmed
to serve: roast potatoes (see tip)
   and broccolini

1 Combine the apricots and orange juice in a bowl; set aside for 20 minutes.
2 Meanwhile, melt butter in a medium skillet over medium heat; add onion and cook, stirring, for 5 minutes or until soft. Stir in bread crumbs; cook for 1 minute or until bread crumbs are golden. Remove from heat; stir in pistachios, sage, and apricot mixture.
3 Preheat a 7-quart air fryer to 400°F/200°C for 5 minutes.
4 Untie and unroll lamb; place, skin-side down, on a cutting board. Using a sharp knife, cut three ½in (1cm) deep slits along the length of the lamb to open up the flesh. Press pistachio mixture along the center of the lamb; roll up to enclose filling. Tie lamb at 1in (2.5cm) intervals with kitchen twine to secure. Rub all over with oil and season.

5 Carefully place lamb and garlic in the air-fryer basket. Reset the temperature to 325°F/170°C; cook for 25 minutes. Turn lamb over and cover with foil; cook for a further 25 minutes for medium or until cooked to your liking.
6 Transfer lamb and garlic to a dish; cover loosely with foil and let rest for 10 minutes.
7 Serve slices of lamb with garlic, warm gravy, roast potatoes, and broccolini.

TIP To roast potatoes, cook 2lb (1kg) halved fingerling potatoes tossed in olive oil at 400°F/200°C for 20 minutes, turning halfway through cooking time, until golden and tender. Season with sea salt flakes to serve.

prep + cook time
1 hour 15 minutes
serves 6

TIP While traditionally
eaten at breakfast,
this Maghrebi dish
can also be enjoyed
as a light dinner.

WHITE BEAN
SHAKSHUKA

2 tbsp finely chopped cilantro stems
2 scallions, finely chopped
½ tsp ground cumin
½ tsp smoked paprika
2 tsp extra-virgin olive oil
1 x 14oz (400g) jar spicy pasta sauce
1 x 15.5ox (440g) can cannellini
    beans, drained, rinsed
1 chargrilled red bell pepper, sliced
4 eggs, at room temperature
salt and pepper to taste
1 medium avocado, diced
to serve: mixed salad greens and
    chargrilled split pita bread

1 Oil a 3-cup (750ml) 8in (20cm) ovenproof dish; ensure the dish will fit into a 5.3-quart air fryer. (You can also use two large ramekins.)
2 Put cilantro stems, scallions, spices, and olive oil in the dish, then place in the air-fryer basket; at 350°F/180°C, cook for 3 minutes until fragrant.
3 Carefully add pasta sauce, beans, and pepper to dish; stir until combined. Cover top of dish with foil; cook for 10 minutes, until mixture is hot.
4 Make four indents in the bean mixture and break an egg into each, then season with salt and freshly ground black pepper; cook for 8 minutes, until eggs are just set or cooked to your liking.
5 Top with avocado and salad greens. Serve with chargrilled pita bread.

**prep + cook time
25 minutes serves 2**

CRACKING PORK BELLY
& ASIAN SALAD

2lb (1kg) piece boneless pork belly,
   rind scored (see tips)
1 tbsp salt flakes
½ tsp Chinese five-spice powder
olive oil for misting
1 cucumber, thinly sliced lengthwise
1 small red onion, thinly sliced
¼ medium napa cabbage, shredded
1 cup (30g) Thai basil leaves
1 cup (30g) cilantro leaves
2 cups (60g) baby spinach
2 long red chilies, seeded,
   thinly sliced
1 scallion, thinly sliced
1 lime (65g), cut into wedges

GINGER DRESSING
1 lemongrass stalk, finely chopped
1 tbsp finely grated fresh ginger
1½ tbsp soy sauce
1½ tbsp lime juice
1 tbsp sesame oil
1 tbsp rice wine vinegar
1 tbsp sugar

1 Preheat a 5.3-quart air fryer to 350°F/180°C for 3 minutes.

2 Pat pork dry with paper towels. Combine half of the sea salt flakes and the five-spice powder; rub into pork rind.

3 Carefully place pork in the air-fryer basket and spray with oil. Reset temperature to 400°F/200°C; cook for 25 minutes, until pork rind crackles.

4 Reset the temperature to 325°F/160°C; cook for a further 30 minutes until pork is tender, or an internal temperature of 160–170°F/70–75°C is reached on a meat thermometer. (Cover pork with foil if overbrowning.)

5 Meanwhile, to make ginger dressing, whisk ingredients in a small bowl.

6 Layer cucumber, onion, cabbage, herbs, spinach, and chili pepper on a platter.

7 Thickly slice pork and place on top of salad. Sprinkle with scallions and with remaining sea salt flakes; drizzle with the dressing. Serve with lime wedges.

TIPS A sharp utility knife or similar is the best tool for scoring the pork rind; alternatively, you can ask your butcher to do it for you. As soon as you get home, place the pork on a sheet pan, uncovered, in the fridge for up to 2 days, to dry out the rind— this will help with crackling the rind.

**prep + cook time
1¼ hours serves 4**

GREEN CURRY CHICKEN
WITH PICKLED RADISH

2 tbsp Thai green curry paste
1 tbsp extra-virgin olive oil
1 tbsp fish sauce
1 tbsp lime juice
1 tbsp light soft brown sugar
4 chicken thighs, skin on
to serve: microwaveable coconut
   rice and finely chopped scallions

PICKLED RADISH
¼ cup (60ml) rice wine vinegar
1 tsp light soft brown sugar
½ tsp sea salt flakes
¼ cup (60ml) cold water
6 mixed radishes, trimmed, thinly
   sliced (see tip)

1 To make pickled radish, combine vinegar, sugar, and salt flakes in a small bowl; add cold water and stir to combine. Add radishes; mix to combine. Set aside until needed.
2 Preheat a 7-quart air fryer to 350°F/180°C for 3 minutes.
3 Combine curry paste, olive oil, fish sauce, lime juice, and sugar in a large bowl; add chicken and turn to coat.
4 Carefully place chicken, skin-side down, in the air-fryer basket; cook for 20 minutes, turning after 8 minutes, or until golden and cooked through. (There will be a little bit of smoke in the initial 5–7 minutes of cooking; however, this will stop with further cooking.)
5 Serve chicken on coconut rice, topped with chopped scallions, and drained pickled radish.

TIP We used a mixture of red and watermelon radishes for the pickle.

prep + cook time
35 minutes serves 4

CHICKEN PARMIGIANA

3 boneless skinless chicken breasts
½ cup (75g) all-purpose flour
salt and pepper to taste
2 eggs
1 garlic clove, crushed
1 tbsp water
1½ cups (110g) panko bread crumbs
1 tsp sweet paprika
2 tsp finely grated lemon zest
1 tbsp finely chopped
    flat-leaf parsley
oil for misting
1 cup (280g) pasta sauce
5oz (180g) mozzarella cheese, sliced
¼ cup (20g) finely grated Parmesan
    cheese
to serve: arugula, roasted vine
    tomatoes (see tip), and lemon
    wedges

1 Cut chicken breasts in half horizontally to make six pieces. Place chicken between two sheets of plastic wrap; pound gently with a rolling pin until even in thickness.

2 Place flour in a small bowl and season. Lightly beat eggs, garlic, and water in a second bowl. Place bread crumbs, paprika, lemon zest, and parsley in a third bowl. Dust chicken in flour, shaking off excess, dip in egg, then coat in bread crumb mixture. Spray chicken generously on both sides with oil.

3 Preheat a 5.3-quart air fryer to 350°F/180°C for 3 minutes.

4 Carefully place three pieces of chicken in the air-fryer basket; cook for 12 minutes until golden brown and cooked through.

Transfer to a sheet pan; cover to keep warm. Repeat cooking with remaining chicken.

5 Return three pieces of chicken to the basket. Top each with 2 tablespoons pasta sauce and half of the mozzarella and Parmesan cheese; cook for 8 minutes until cheeses are melted and bubbling. Repeat with remaining chicken, pasta sauce, and cheeses.

6 Serve chicken with arugula, roasted tomatoes, and lemon wedges.

prep + cook time 1 hour makes 6

TIP To roast vine tomatoes, add them to the edge of the basket with the escalopes in step 5; cook for 6 minutes.

CHEAT'S SAUSAGE CASSOULET

1lb (500g) thick pork sausages
olive oil for misting
1 tbsp extra-virgin olive oil
1 medium onion, finely chopped
2 slices thick-cut bacon, thinly sliced
2 garlic cloves, crushed
1 medium red bell pepper, coarsely
    chopped
1 medium zucchini, coarsely
    chopped
8oz (250g) roma tomatoes
½ cup (125ml) dry red wine
1½ cups (390g) pasta sauce
3 sprigs of thyme
1 x 15oz (425g) can lima beans,
    drained, rinsed
1½ cups (105g) coarse fresh
    sourdough bread crumbs
⅓ cup (25g) grated Gruyère cheese
⅓ cup (20g) chopped
    flat-leaf parsley
to serve: sea salt flakes

1 Preheat a 7-quart air fryer to 400°F/200°C for 3 minutes.

2 Spray sausages with oil. Carefully place sausages in the air-fryer basket; cook for 8 minutes, turning halfway through cooking time, or until browned.

3 Meanwhile, heat oil in a large skillet over medium-high heat; cook onion and bacon, stirring, for 5 minutes or until onion is softened and bacon is crisp. Add garlic, pepper, and zucchini; cook, stirring, for 4 minutes or until vegetables are lightly browned. Add tomatoes and wine; bring to a boil. Add pasta sauce and thyme; return to a boil.

4 Transfer sausages to a board and coarsely chop; add to tomato mixture with lima beans. Transfer mixture to a deep 8in (20cm) round ovenproof dish.

5 Carefully wipe the air-fryer basket clean; place the ovenproof dish in the basket. Reset the temperature to 350°F/180°C; cook for 8 minutes.

6 Meanwhile, combine bread crumbs, Gruyère, and parsley in a bowl.

7 Top cassoulet with bread crumb mixture, spray with oil, then press crumbs down firmly; cook for 5 minutes until bread crumbs are golden.

8 Sprinkle cassoulet with sea salt flakes to serve.

**prep + cook time
40 minutes serves 4**

171

SOUTHERN FRIED CHICKEN

1 whole chicken, about 3¼lb (1.6kg) (see tip)
1 cup (250ml) buttermilk
1 egg, lightly beaten
salt and pepper to taste
1¼ cups (185g) all-purpose flour
2 tsp smoked paprika
1 tsp garlic powder
1 tsp onion flakes
1 tsp dried oregano
1 tsp sea salt flakes
1 tsp ground cumin
½ tsp chili powder
olive oil for misting
to serve: extra sea salt flakes, mayonnaise, and hot sauce

1 Using a sharp knife, cut chicken into eight pieces. Make two deep slits through the thickest part of the meat to the bone in each chicken piece.
2 Combine buttermilk and egg in a large bowl, then season; add chicken and turn to coat. Cover bowl. Refrigerate for 6 hours or overnight.
3 Combine flour, paprika, garlic powder, onion flakes, oregano, salt, cumin, and chili powder in a large bowl; season.
4 Working with one piece of chicken at a time, drain excess buttermilk mixture, then roll chicken in flour mixture to coat. Repeat with remaining chicken and flour mixture; spray generously all over with oil.
5 Preheat a 7-quart air fryer to 400°F/200°C for 3 minutes.

6 Carefully line the air-fryer basket with a silicone mat, if available (see page 11). Place chicken in the basket; at 400°F/200°C, cook for 10 minutes.
7 Turn chicken over. Reset the temperature to 350°F/180°C; cook for 10 minutes or until crisp and cooked through. (The breast pieces may cook a little quicker than the thighs and legs.)
8 Sprinkle chicken with extra sea salt flakes. Serve with mayonnaise swirled with a little hot sauce.

**prep + cook time
40 minutes
(+ refrigeration)
serves 4**

TIP You could also use
3¼lb (1.6kg) chicken
pieces on the bone; you
may need to adjust the
cooking time depending
on the pieces.

AIR
BAKE

The air fryer isn't just about savory
food; it's also great for baking sweet
treats. Make all your favorite baked
recipes, such as cakes, muffins,
brownies, cookies, tarts, pies, and
more—including a couple
of savory options.

CHOCOLATE CAKE
WITH FUDGE ICING

½ cup (125g) butter, softened
1 tsp vanilla extract
¾ cup (165g) sugar
2 eggs
1⅓ cups (185g) all-purpose flour
1 tsp baking powder
½ tsp baking soda
½ tsp salt
½ cup (50g) unsweetened
   cocoa powder
½ cup (125ml) milk

FUDGE ICING
4 tbsp (60g) cold butter, chopped
⅓ cup (75g) firmly packed
   light soft brown sugar
1 tbsp milk
1 cup (160g) powdered sugar
2 tbsp cocoa powder

1 Preheat a 7-quart air fryer to 325°F/160°C for 5 minutes. Grease a deep 8in (20cm) round cake pan; line bottom and side of pan with parchment paper.
2 Beat butter, vanilla, sugar, and eggs, sifted flour, baking powder, baking soda, salt, cocoa, and milk in a large bowl with an electric mixer on low speed until combined. Increase speed to medium; beat for 3 minutes or until mixture is smooth and paler in color. Spoon mixture into cake pan. Cover pan with a piece of greased foil.
3 Carefully place cake pan in the air-fryer basket; cook for 1 hour until a skewer inserted into the center comes out clean. Remove from the basket. Leave cake in pan for 10 minutes before turning, top-side up, onto a wire rack to cool.

4 Meanwhile, to make fudge icing, stir butter, brown sugar, and milk in a small saucepan over low heat, until sugar dissolves. Remove from heat. Sift powdered sugar and cocoa powder into a small bowl; gradually whisk in hot butter mixture until smooth. Cover bowl. Refrigerate for 40 minutes or until icing thickens.
5 Beat icing with a wooden spoon until spreadable. Spread top of cooled cake with fudge icing.

**prep + cook time
1¼ hours
(+ refrigeration)
serves 12**

TIP Make sure that you are wearing a long-sleeved top while piping the churros mixture into the hot air-fryer basket, as this will protect you from touching the hot sides.

CHURROS
WITH CHOCOLATE SAUCE

4 tbsp (60g) butter
pinch of sea salt flakes
½ cup (125ml) cold water
⅓ cup (75g) sugar
½ cup (75g) all-purpose flour
2 eggs, lightly beaten
olive oil for misting
1 tsp ground cinnamon
4oz (125g) dark (semi-sweet)
   chocolate, chopped
½ cup (125ml) heavy cream

1 Bring butter, salt, cold water, and 1 tablespoon of the sugar to a boil in a medium saucepan. Add sifted flour; beat with a wooden spoon over high heat until mixture comes away from the bottom and side of the pan to form a smooth ball. Transfer to a small bowl; beat in eggs, in two batches, with a wooden spoon until mixture becomes glossy. Spoon into a piping bag fitted with a ¾in (2cm) fluted tube.

2 Preheat a 7-quart air fryer to 350°F/180°C for 3 minutes.

3 Spray the air-fryer basket with oil. Carefully pipe four 4in (10cm) lengths of batter, 2in (5cm) apart, into the basket (see tip); cook for 12 minutes, until golden and crisp. Repeat cooking with remaining batter to make a total of 8 churros.

4 Meanwhile, to make cinnamon sugar, combine cinnamon and remaining sugar in a shallow bowl. Immediately place hot churros in cinnamon sugar and toss to coat.

5 To make chocolate sauce, place chocolate and cream in a small saucepan over low-medium heat; stir until smooth and combined.

6 Serve churros with warm chocolate sauce.

**prep + cook time
45 minutes makes 8**

LEMON CURD SCONES

2¾ cups (375g) all-purpose flour
2 tsp baking powder
½ tsp baking soda
½ tsp salt
2 tbsp sugar
1¼ cup 300ml buttermilk
¼ cup (80g) lemon curd
olive oil for misting
to serve: fruit jam and
   whipped cream

1 Sift flour, baking powder, baking soda, salt, and sugar into a large bowl. Make a well in the center; pour in combined buttermilk and lemon curd. Using a flat-bladed knife, gently stir until dough just comes together.
2 Turn out dough onto a lightly floured work surface. Using your hands, briefly knead. Pat out until dough is 1¼in (3cm) thick.
3 Using a floured cutter, cut 2¼in (5.5cm) rounds from dough. Press scraps of dough together until 1¼in (3cm) thick. Repeat cutting to get a total of 9 scones. Brush top of scones with any buttermilk left in the carton or with 1 tablespoon milk.
4 Preheat a 7-quart air fryer to 350°F/180°C for 3 minutes.
5 Spray the air-fryer basket with oil. Carefully, place scones, side by side, in the basket. Reset the temperature to 325°F/160°C; cook for 17 minutes.
6 Serve warm scones with jam and cream.

**prep + cook time
35 minutes makes 9**

SERVE IT You can also serve the scones with lemon curd and whipped cream, if you like.

PEANUT BUTTER BROWNIES

½ cup (125g) butter, chopped
6½oz (200g) dark chocolate
   (at least 45% cocoa solids),
   chopped
½ cup (110g) sugar
½ cup (160g) caramel sauce
¼ cup (70g) crunchy peanut butter
2 eggs, lightly beaten
1⅓ cup (150g) all-purpose flour
1 tsp baking powder
½ tsp salt
1 tbsp unsweetened cocoa powder

1 Stir butter and chocolate in a medium saucepan over low heat until just smooth. Remove from heat; stir in sugar. Let cool for 10 minutes.

2 Preheat a 7-quart air fryer to 325°F/160°C for 5 minutes. Grease a 8in (20cm) square cake pan; line bottom and sides with parchment paper.

3 Microwave caramel sauce for 30 seconds or until softened; stir in the peanut butter.

4 Stir eggs into chocolate mixture, then sifted flour, baking powder, baking soda, salt, and cocoa. Spread half of the brownie mixture into the cake pan; dollop with half of the peanut butter mixture.

Gently spread remaining brownie mixture over the top, then dollop with remaining peanut butter mixture. Using a skewer, swirl the peanut butter mixture through the brownie mixture. Cover pan tightly with foil.

5 Carefully place cake pan in the air-fryer basket; at 325°F/160°C, cook for 25 minutes.

6 Remove foil; cook for a further 10 minutes or until brownie is just set on top. Remove from the basket. Let brownie cool in pan.

7 Cut brownie into 12 pieces.

**prep + cook time
55 minutes makes 12**

CARAMELIZED ONION, DILL & CARAWAY SAUSAGE ROLLS

1lb (450g) ground pork
1 cup (100g) packaged bread
   crumbs
1 egg, lightly beaten
2 garlic cloves, crushed
¼ cup finely chopped dill
1 tbsp caraway seeds, plus
   1 tsp extra
½ cup (150g) caramelized onion
   jam or chutney
2 tsp malt vinegar
salt and pepper to taste
3 sheets of frozen puff pastry,
   just thawed
2 egg yolks
1 tsp water
oil for misting
to serve: steak sauce or
   barbecue sauce

1 Preheat a 5.3-quart air fryer to 350°F/180°C for 3 minutes.

2 Combine ground pork, bread crumbs, egg, garlic, dill, the 1 tablespoon caraway seeds, jam, and vinegar in a large bowl; season well.

3 Cut pastry sheets in half. Spoon or pipe pork mixture in a line through the center of each pastry piece; roll pastry over to enclose filling. Cut each roll into four pieces; place, seam-side down, on a sheet pan lined with parchment paper. Combine egg yolks and water in a small bowl. Brush pastry with egg and sprinkle with extra caraway seeds.

4 Spray the air-fryer basket with oil. Carefully place 8 sausage rolls in the basket; cook for 15 minutes until puffed and cooked through. Transfer to a wire rack. Repeat cooking two more times with the remaining sausage rolls.

5 Serve hot sausage rolls with sauce.

PREP IT Sausage rolls can be prepared to the end of step 3 a day ahead; refrigerate until ready to bake.

KEEP IT Sausage rolls can be frozen in an airtight container for up to 3 months.

prep + cook time
1 hour makes 24

STRAWBERRY
POP TARTS

8oz (225g) strawberries,
    finely chopped
2 tbsp strawberry jam
1 tbsp cornstarch
4 sheets of frozen pie crust,
    just thawed
1 egg, lightly beaten
½ cup (80g) powdered sugar
2 tsp cold water
pink food coloring, to tint
to decorate: candy sprinkles

1 Combine strawberries, jam, and cornstarch in a small bowl. Cut each pie crust sheet into six 3¼in x 4in (8cm x 10cm) rectangles. Place a level tablespoon of strawberry mixture in the center of half of the rectangles. Brush edges with a little egg. Cover filling with remaining rectangles; using a fork, press edges together to seal.
2 Preheat a 7-quart air fryer to 350°F/180°C for 3 minutes.
3 Carefully place half of the tarts in the air-fryer basket; cook for 12 minutes, turning after 10 minutes of cooking time, until crust is golden and cooked. Transfer to a wire rack to cool. Repeat cooking with remaining tarts.
4 Combine powdered sugar, the cold water, and food coloring in a small bowl. Spoon icing over cooled tarts; sprinkle immediately with candy sprinkles. Let stand until icing sets.

prep + cook time
35 minutes (+ standing)
makes 12

BERRY FRANGIPANE GALETTE

1 cup (150g) all-purpose flour
2 tbsp sugar
4 tbsp (60g) chilled butter, chopped
1 egg yolk
2 tbsp ground almonds
4½oz (150g) frozen mixed berries
2 tsp cornstarch
to serve: powdered sugar and ice
   cream

FRANGIPANE FILLING
4 tbsp (60g) butter, softened
¼ cup (55g) sugar
1 tsp vanilla extract
1 egg yolk
⅔ cup (80g) ground almonds
1½ tbsp all-purpose flour

1 To make pastry, process flour, sugar, and butter in a food processor until mixture resembles fine bread crumbs. Add egg yolk; process until dough just comes together. Turn out onto a work surface and shape into a disc; wrap in plastic wrap. Refrigerate for 30 minutes.

2 Meanwhile, to make frangipane filling, beat butter, sugar, and vanilla in a small bowl with an electric mixer until pale and creamy. Beat in egg yolk until combined. Stir in ground almonds and flour until combined.

3 Preheat a 7-quart air fryer to 350°F/180°C for 5 minutes.

4 Roll out pastry between two sheets of parchment paper until ⅛in (3mm) thick. Using a plate or cake pan, cut out a 10in (25cm) round from pastry; discard scraps. Sprinkle ground almonds over pastry round, then evenly spread with frangipane, leaving a 1in (3cm) border. Toss berries in cornstarch to coat, shaking off excess; sprinkle over frangipane. Fold pastry border up and over filling.

5 Using the parchment as an aid, carefully lower the galette into the air-fryer basket, then cover basket tightly with foil; cook for 30 minutes.

6 Remove foil. Reset the temperature to 325°F/160°C; cook for a further 15–18 minutes until pastry is golden and frangipane is cooked through. Using the parchment as an aid, carefully lift the galette from the basket.

7 Dust with powdered sugar and serve with ice cream.

prep + cook time
1 hour 10 minutes
(+ refrigeration)
serves 6

APPLEY PIE ROLLS

3/4lb (400g) granny smith apples, peeled cored, and chopped
¼ cup (40g) golden raisins
1½ tbsp sugar
½ tsp ground cinnamon
1½ tbsp ground almonds
8 x 8¾in (21.5cm) frozen spring roll wrappers, thawed (see tip)
olive oil for misting
to serve: powdered sugar, to dust, and vanilla ice cream

1 Combine apples, raisins, sugar, cinnamon, and ground almonds in a medium bowl.
2 Place a spring roll wrapper on a clean work surface. Place 2 level tablespoons of apple filling in a line a third up from the bottom edge, leaving a 1½in (4cm) border on each side. Fold bottom of wrapper over filling once, fold in the sides, then roll up to enclose filling; brush the join with a little water to seal. Repeat with remaining spring roll wrappers and filling to make 8 rolls in total.
3 Preheat a 7-quart air fryer to 400°F/200°C for 3 minutes.

4 Spray rolls generously all over with oil. Carefully place rolls in the air-fryer basket; cook for 15 minutes until golden brown.
5 Dust rolls with powdered sugar and serve with ice cream.

**prep + cook time
35 minutes makes 8**

TIP You can find spring roll wrappers in the freezer section of Asian grocers or supermarkets.

KEEP IT Cookies will
keep in an airtight
container for up to
2 weeks.

BASIC VANILLA BUTTER COOKIES

½ cup (125g) butter, softened
½ cup (110g) sugar, plus 2 tbsp extra
1 tsp vanilla extract
1 egg yolk
1½ cups (185g) all-purpose flour
to serve: powdered sugar, to dust

1 Beat butter, the ½ cup sugar, and vanilla in a small bowl with an electric mixer until light and fluffy. Beat in egg yolk until combined. Sift flour, in two batches, into butter mixture; mix well.
2 Knead dough on a lightly floured surface until smooth. Using your hands, shape dough into a 10in (25cm) long log. Place the extra 2 tablespoons sugar on a plate; roll log in the sugar. Wrap log in parchment paper. Freeze for 1 hour or until firm.
3 Remove log from the freezer. Let stand for 10 minutes. Slice into 15 rounds, each about ¾in (1.5cm) thick.
4 Preheat a 7-quart air fryer to 325°F/160°C for 5 minutes.

5 Carefully line the air-fryer basket with parchment paper. Place half of the cookies, ¾in (2cm) apart, in the basket (place remaining cookies in the fridge until needed); at 350°F/160°C, cook for 12 minutes until golden. Remove the basket from the air-fryer pan. Leave cookies in the basket for 10 minutes before transferring to a wire rack to cool completely. Repeat cooking with remaining cookies.
6 Dust cookies with powdered sugar.

**prep + cook time
40 minutes (+ freezing, standing & cooling)
makes 15**

TRIPLE-CHOC

Add ⅓ cup (80g) each of milk, dark, and white chocolate chips to 1 quantity Basic Vanilla Butter Cookies recipe (page 193) just before adding the flour in step 1. Roll level tablespoons of mixture into balls. Flatten balls until ½in (1cm) thick. Freeze for 20 minutes. Bake as recipe directs in steps 4 and 5.

TIP You could also use 5½oz (180g) hand-chopped chocolate of a single type, if you like.

ORANGE & PECAN

Add 1 tsp finely grated orange zest and ½ cup (60g) chopped toasted pecans to 1 quantity Basic Vanilla Butter Cookies recipe (page 193) just before adding the flour in step 1. Continue with the recipe from step 2.

COOKIES

SPICED MAPLE

Add ½ tsp cinnamon, ¼ tsp allspice, and ¼ tsp nutmeg to 1 quantity Basic Vanilla Butter Cookies recipe (page 193) when adding the flour in step 1. Continue with the recipe from step 2. To make maple icing, combine ¾ cup (90g) sifted powdered sugar, 1½ tbsp maple syrup, and 3 tsp water; beat with a wooden spoon until icing is smooth and a pouring consistency. Drizzle icing on top of cooled cookies.

4 WAYS

LEMON & CRANBERRY

Add 1 tsp finely grated lemon zest and ½ cup (65g) dried cranberries to 1 quantity Basic Vanilla Butter Cookies recipe (page 193) just before adding the flour in step 1. Continue with the recipe from step 2.

TRIPLE-CHOC COOKIES

ORANGE & PECAN COOKIES

LEMON & CRANBERRY COOKIES

SPICED MAPLE COOKIES

CHOCOLATE LAVA CAKES

2 tbsp (30g) butter, softened, plus
   ½ cup (125g) butter, chopped
2 tbsp unsweetened cocoa powder
1 cup (170g) semi-sweet
   chocolate chips
2 eggs
2 egg yolks
⅓ cup (75g) sugar
¼ cup (35g) all-purpose flour
to serve: extra cocoa powder, to
   dust, and coffee ice cream

1 Grease six ¾-cup (180ml) ovenproof dishes (ramekins) with the 2 tbsp softened butter; dust with cocoa, shaking off excess.
2 Stir chocolate and the extra ½ cup chopped butter in a small saucepan over low heat until smooth. Let cool for 10 minutes. Transfer mixture to a large bowl.
3 Beat eggs, egg yolks, and sugar in a small bowl with an electric mixer until thick and creamy. Fold egg mixture and sifted flour into barely warm chocolate mixture. Spoon mixture into ramekins.
4 Preheat a 7-quart air fryer to 350°F/180°C for 3 minutes.
5 Carefully place dishes in the air-fryer basket; cook for 10–12 minutes. Remove from the basket.

Leave cakes in the ramekins for 1 minute before gently inverting onto serving plates.
6 Dust cakes with extra cocoa and serve immediately with ice cream.

TIPS These cakes should be served shortly after they come out of the air fryer. If they are allowed to sit for longer than 1 minute, the gooey center will firm up and the chocolate won't ooze out when they're cut. Warning: the melted chocolate center will be hot, so be careful when biting into the cake.

**prep + cook time
30 minutes (+ cooling)
serves 6**

CHOCOLATE CANNOLI
WITH HAZELNUT CREAM

---

1 cup (150g) all-purpose flour
1 tbsp cocoa powder
1 tbsp sugar
1 egg
1 egg yolk
1 tbsp marsala wine
2 tsp olive oil
2 tsp cold water
1 egg white, lightly beaten
olive oil for misting
to serve: powdered sugar and fresh
    raspberries

HAZELNUT CREAM
1 cup (250ml) heavy cream
2 tbsp powdered sugar
4oz (125g) mascarpone
¼ cup (85g) hazelnut chocolate
    spread

1 Process flour, cocoa, and sugar until just combined. Add egg, egg yolk, marsala wine, oil, and the cold water; process until dough starts to come together. Turn out onto a lightly floured surface; knead until smooth. Divide dough in half and shape into two discs; wrap in plastic wrap. Refrigerate for 1 hour.
2 Roll out one dough disc on a lightly floured surface until 2mm thick (alternatively, roll dough through a pasta machine). Using a 4in (10cm) round cutter, cut out six rounds, rerolling the scraps if necessary. Wrap each round around an ungreased metal cannoli mold (see tip), overlapping ends slightly. Brush ends with a little egg white to secure (ensure you don't get egg white on the molds; otherwise, the dough will stick to them once cooked). Repeat with remaining dough disc to make 12 cannoli shells in total.
3 Preheat a 7-quart air fryer to 400°F/200°C for 3 minutes.
4 Spray cannoli all over with olive oil. Carefully, line the air-fryer basket with parchment paper. Place cannoli in the basket; cook for 7 minutes, turning halfway through cooking time, or until golden. Using tongs, transfer to a plate to cool slightly. Carefully remove molds from warm cannoli. Let cool.
5 Meanwhile, to make hazelnut cream, beat cream and powdered sugar in a small bowl with an electric mixer until soft peaks form. Add mascarpone and hazelnut chocolate spread; beat for 20 seconds or until just combined. Spoon cream mixture into a piping bag fitted with a ½in (1cm) plain nozzle. Pipe hazelnut cream into cooled cannoli shells.
6 Dust cannoli with powdered sugar. Serve with raspberries.

TIP Cannelloni pasta shells can be used instead of speciality metal cannoli molds; however, you will need to grease them first. Ensure that you wrap the dough rounds loosely around the pasta shells, to make removing them easier.

**prep + cook time
45 minutes
(+ refrigeration) makes 12**

KEEP IT Tart will
keep in an airtight
container in the fridge
for up to 3 days.

TANGY LEMON TART

½ cup (125g) butter, coarsely
   chopped
¼ cup (40g) powdered sugar
1¼ cups (185g) all-purpose flour
3 eggs
1 cup (220g) sugar, plus 2 tbsp extra
2 tsp finely grated lemon zest
½ cup (125ml) lemon juice
oil for misting
1 medium lemon, thinly sliced
to serve: extra powdered sugar,
   to dust

1 Preheat a 5.3-quart air fryer to 350°F/180°C for 3 minutes. Grease an 8in (20cm) loose-bottomed tart pan.

2 Beat butter and powdered sugar in a small bowl with an electric mixer until smooth. Stir in 1 cup (150g) of the flour until a dough forms. Press mixture evenly over bottom and up the side of tart pan. Fold a length of foil into a long strip; place under tart pan to act as a sling.

3 Carefully lower tart pan, on the sling, into the air-fryer basket; cook for 10 minutes.

4 Using the back of a spoon, press crust back down over the bottom and up the side of tart pan; cook for a further 8 minutes until tart base is dry and lightly golden.

5 Meanwhile, to make lemon filling, place eggs, the 1 cup of sugar, remaining flour, and the lemon zest and juice in a medium saucepan; whisk continuously over medium heat until mixture boils and thickens.

6 Ladle hot filling mixture into the hot tart base in the basket. Reset the temperature to 325°F/160°C; cook for 3–5 minutes until filling is set. Using the foil sling as an aid, lift from the basket and place on a wire rack. Leave tart in pan to cool.

7 Meanwhile, spray the basket with oil. Sprinkle lemon slices with the extra 2 tbsp sugar and place in the basket; cook for 6 minutes, until caramelized.

8 To serve, top tart with caramelized lemon slices and dust with extra powdered sugar.

**prep + cook time
45 minutes serves 8**

MEGA CARROT CAKE MUFFINS

2 cups (240g) ground almonds
2 tbsp chia seeds
1 tsp baking powder (see tip)
½ tsp baking soda
1 tsp ground cinnamon
1 tbsp ground ginger
3 eggs
¼ cup (60ml) extra-virgin olive oil
¾ cup (110g) coconut sugar
2 tsp vanilla extract
1 large zucchini
1 large carrot
1 large apple
½ cup (120g) smooth ricotta
¼ cup (40g) natural almonds, chopped

1 Preheat a 5.3-quart air fryer to 325°F/160°C for 3 minutes. Triple-layer 18 muffin cup liners to make six thick liners.
2 Combine ground almonds, chia seeds, baking powder, baking soda, and spices in a large bowl. Whisk eggs, oil, coconut sugar, and vanilla in a medium bowl; add to dry ingredients, stirring until just combined.
3 Coarsely grate zucchini, carrot, and apple into a medium bowl. Using your hands, pick up handfuls of the zucchini mixture and squeeze very firmly to remove excess liquid. Fold zucchini mixture into almond mixture until just combined. Divide muffin mixture evenly among muffin cups.
4 Carefully place muffin cups in the air-fryer basket; cook for 5 minutes.

5 Cover top of muffins with a piece of foil; cook for a further 25 minutes.
6 Top each muffin with a spoonful of ricotta and sprinkle with chopped almonds; cook for 5 minutes until ricotta is browned and a skewer inserted into the center of a muffin comes out clean. Transfer to a wire rack to cool.

KEEP IT Muffins will keep in an airtight container in the fridge for up to 1 week, or they can be frozen for up to 2 months.

TIP To make gluten-free muffins, use a gluten-free brand of baking powder.

**prep + cook time
45 minutes makes 6**

LEMON CURD & RASPBERRY
BREAD & BUTTER PUDDING

8oz (250g) crusty sourdough bread,
  thickly sliced
½ cup (160g) lemon curd
1 cup (250ml) heavy cream
¾ cup (180ml) milk
3 eggs
¼ cup (55g) sugar
1 tsp vanilla extract
4oz (125g) frozen raspberries
to serve: extra lemon curd

1 Grease a 1.5-quart (6-cup), 8in (20cm) round baking dish; ensure the dish will fit into a 7-quart air fryer.
2 Spread bread slices thickly with lemon curd. Arrange bread, curd-side up, in dish.
3 To make custard, combine cream and milk in a microwave-safe bowl; heat in microwave on HIGH (100%) for 2 minutes or until warm. Whisk eggs, sugar, and vanilla in a bowl until combined; gradually whisk in warm cream mixture until combined.
4 Pour custard over bread slices in dish; top with raspberries. Using a spatula, press bread down gently to submerge in the custard. Let stand for 5 minutes. Cover dish tightly with foil.
5 Preheat air fryer to 300°F/150°C for 5 minutes.
6 Carefully place dish in the air-fryer basket; cook for 30 minutes.
7 Remove foil. Reset the temperature to 325°F/160°C; cook for a further 12 minutes until golden and just set. Remove from the basket. Let pudding stand for 5 minutes to cool slightly.
8 Serve pudding dolloped with extra lemon curd.

**prep + cook time
1 hour serves 12**

TIP Homemade pesto can be replaced with ¼ cup (65g) jarred basil or sun-dried tomato pesto.

CHEESY PESTO SCROLLS

1 cup (50g) firmly packed
  basil leaves
1 garlic clove, chopped
2 tbsp pine nuts, toasted
2 tbsp finely grated Parmesan
  cheese
¼ cup (60ml) extra-virgin olive oil
1 tbsp lemon juice
salt and pepper to taste
2¼ cups (300g) all-purose flour
2 tsp baking powder
½ tsp baking soda
1 tsp salt
1 tbsp sugar
4 tbsp (60g) cold butter,
  coarsely chopped
about ¾ cup (180ml) milk

CHEESY FILLING
½ cup (60g) grated mozzarella
  cheese
¼ cup (35g) grated Cheddar cheese
¼ cup (25g) grated Parmesan
  cheese

1 To make pesto, process basil, garlic, pine nuts, and Parmesan cheese in a food processor until chopped finely. With motor operating, gradually add combined oil and lemon juice until pesto is almost smooth; season with salt and freshly ground black pepper.

2 Sift flour, baking powder, baking soda, and salt into a medium bowl; stir in sugar. Using your fingers, rub in butter. Add enough milk to form a soft, sticky dough. Turn out onto a lightly floured sheet of parchment paper; lightly knead until smooth. Sprinkle parchment with more flour, if needed. Roll out dough into a 12in x 16in (30cm x 40cm) rectangle.

3 Spread dough evenly with the pesto. Sprinkle cheeses for filling evenly over pesto. Roll up dough tightly from a long side to form a log; place log in the freezer for 10 minutes to firm slightly.

4 Preheat a 7-quart air fryer to 325°F/160°C for 5 minutes.

5 Using a serrated knife, trim ends off the log; cut into 12 slices.

6 Carefully line the air-fryer basket with parchment paper. Place scrolls, cut-side up, in the basket, then cover basket tightly with foil; cook for 10 minutes.

7 Remove foil; cook for a further 10 minutes, until scrolls are golden and cooked through.

8 Serve scrolls warm or cold.

prep + cook time
50 minutes (+ freezing)
makes 12

PASSION FRUIT BUTTERMILK CAKE

½ cup (125g) butter
1 cup (220g) sugar
2 tsp vanilla extract
2 eggs
2¼ cups (300g) all-purpose flour
2 tsp baking power
½ tsp baking soda
1 tsp salt
⅔ cup (160ml) buttermilk
¾ cup (180ml) passion fruit pulp (see tip)
1½ cups (240g) powdered sugar

1 Preheat a 7-quart air fryer to 325°F/160°C for 5 minutes. Grease a deep 8in (20cm) round springform cake pan; line bottom and side of pan with parchment paper. Ensure that the pan will fit into the air fryer.

2 Beat butter, sugar, and vanilla in a bowl with an electric mixer until thick and creamy. Beat in eggs, one at a time, until combined. Fold in flour, baking powder, baking soda, salt, buttermilk, and ¼ cup (60ml) of the passion fruit pulp. Spoon mixture into cake pan; cover with foil.

3 Carefully place cake pan in the air-fryer basket; cook for 30 minutes.

4 Remove foil; cook for a further 30 minutes, or until a skewer inserted into the center comes out clean. Remove from the basket. Leave cake in pan for 10 minutes before turning out onto a wire rack to cool.

5 To make passion fruit icing, combine powdered sugar and remaining passion fruit pulp in a small bowl. Spread top of cooled cake with icing.

TIP You will need about 9 passion fruit for this recipe.

prep + cook time
1¼ hours (+ cooling)
serves 12

BANANA FRITTERS
WITH SALTED CARAMEL SAUCE

---

1 tbsp (15g) butter, chopped
1½ cups (110g) panko bread crumbs
½ cup (40g) shredded coconut
½ cup (75g) all-purpose flour
2 eggs
¼ cup (60ml) milk
4 ripe bananas, halved lengthwise
to serve: vanilla ice cream

SALTED CARAMEL SAUCE
½ cup (125ml) heavy cream
½ cup (110g) firmly packed light
  soft brown sugar
2 tbsp (30g) butter, chopped
1 tsp sea salt flakes

1 Melt butter in a medium skillet over medium-high heat. Add bread crumbs and coconut; cook, stirring, for 2 minutes, or until bread crumbs are lightly browned. Transfer to a plate to cool.

2 Place flour on a plate. Whisk eggs and milk together in a medium shallow bowl. Dust bananas in flour, shaking off excess, dip in egg mixture, then coat in bread crumb mixture. Refrigerate for 15 minutes.

3 Preheat a 7-quart air fryer to 350°F/180°C for 3 minutes.

4 Carefully, place fritters in the air-fryer basket; cook for 8 minutes, turning halfway through cooking time, or until golden.

5 Meanwhile, to make salted caramel sauce, stir ingredients, except salt, in a small saucepan over a low heat, without boiling, until sugar dissolves. Bring to a boil, then reduce heat; simmer for 3 minutes or until slightly thickened. Remove from heat and stir in salt.

6 Serve fritters with ice cream, drizzled with salted caramel sauce.

prep + cook time
25 minutes
(+ refrigeration)
serves 4

BANANA BREAD

½ cup (125g) butter, softened
1 cup (220g) firmly packed light soft
    brown sugar
1 tsp vanilla extract
2 eggs
1½ cups (350g) mashed ripe banana
    (see tip)
¼ cup (60ml) maple syrup
1⅔ cups (250g) all-purpose flour
1 tsp baking powder
1 tsp baking soda
1½ tsp ground cinnamon
¼ tsp sea salt flakes
½ cup (25g) coarsely chopped
    roasted walnuts
2 small bananas (130g each),
    halved lengthwise
2 tbsp sugar
to serve: soft ricotta and honey

1 Grease a 4in x 8in (10.5cm x 20cm) loaf pan; line bottom and sides with parchment paper, ensuring parchment sits flush with the rim.
2 Beat butter, brown sugar, and vanilla in a medium bowl with an electric mixer until pale and fluffy. Beat in eggs, one at a time, until just combined, then mashed banana and maple syrup. Sift over flour, baking powder, baking soda, cinnamon, and salt. Add walnuts; stir with a large spoon until combined. Spoon mixture into loaf pan; smooth surface.
3 Preheat a 5.3-quart air fryer to 325°F/160°C for 3 minutes.
4 Carefully, place loaf pan in the air-fryer basket; at 325°F/160°C, cook for 10 minutes.

5 Place banana halves, cut-side up, on top of bread. Cover loaf pan with foil and pierce the foil; cook for 40 minutes.
6 Remove foil; cook for another 5 minutes, until a skewer inserted into the center comes out clean. Remove from the basket. Leave bread in pan for 10 minutes before turning out, top-side up, onto a wire rack to cool. Sprinkle top with sugar while hot.
7 Serve slices of banana bread topped with ricotta and drizzled with honey.

TIP You will need 3 large bananas to make 1½ cups mashed banana.

**prep + cook time
1¼ hours serves 8**

BERRY BAKED PANCAKE

olive oil for misting
1 cup (150g) all-purpose flour
¼ cup (55g) sugar
¼ tsp baking soda
⅔ cup (160ml) buttermilk
1 egg, lightly beaten
2 tsp vanilla extract
2 tbsp (30g) butter, melted
1½oz (50g) blueberries
1½oz (50g) raspberries
to serve: powdered sugar and
    maple syrup

1 Preheat a 7-quart air fryer to 350°F/180°C for 3 minutes. Spray a nonstick 7¼in (18cm) round, 1in (2.5cm) deep pizza pan (see tip) with oil.
2 Place flour, sugar, and baking soda in a large bowl; stir to combine. Whisk buttermilk, egg, vanilla, and butter in a medium bowl. Add buttermilk mixture to flour mixture, stirring until just combined. Spread mixture into pizza pan and smooth; top with berries, pressing them in gently.

3 Carefully place pizza pan in the air-fryer basket; cook for 15 minutes until a skewer inserted into the center comes out clean.
4 Dust warm pancake with powdered sugar and serve with maple syrup.

TIP Many air fryers come with an accessory pack that includes a pizza pan.

**prep + cook time
30 minutes serves 4**

COOKIE PIE

1 frozen pie crust
5 tbsp (70g) butter, softened
⅔ cup (150g) firmly packed
   light soft brown sugar
1 egg
1 tsp vanilla extract
1¼ cup (150g) all-purpose flour
1 tsp baking powder
¼ tsp baking soda
½ tsp salt
¼ cup (45g) semi-sweet
   chocolate chips
¾ cup (110g) assorted chocolate
   candies (see tip)
to serve: powdered sugar

1 Preheat a 5.3-quart air fryer to 340°F/170°C for 3 minutes.

2 Cover pie crust with foil, then weigh foil down with two metal spoons. Carefully place pie crust in the air-fryer basket; cook for 10 minutes until pie crust is lightly golden and dry. Transfer to a cutting board to cool.

3 Meanwhile, to make chocolate chip cookie filling, beat butter, sugar, egg, and vanilla in a small bowl with an electric mixer for 6 minutes or until light and creamy. Stir in sifted flour, baking powder, baking soda, and salt, then chocolate chips.

4 Fill pie crust with the filling; smooth surface. Press assorted chocolates and candies into top of pie. Place pie in the basket; cover with foil.

5 Reset the temperature to 325°F/160°C; cook for 30 minutes, until a skewer inserted into the center of the pie comes out with a few crumbs attached and top is browned and puffed.

6 Serve pie warm or cool, dusted with powdered sugar.

TIP For pie one (top left) we used candy-coated chocolates, caramel-filled chocolate rolls, and chocolate nonpareils. For pie two (top right) we used sliced liquorice candy, caramel-filled chocolate rolls, unicorn confetti, and strawberry-flavored candy sticks. For pie three (bottom) we used candy-coated chocolates, caramel-filled chocolate rolls, chocolate pretzels, cake decorations, and mini letter cookies. Use your imagination and get creative.

SERVE IT Serve with scoops of vanilla ice cream.

prep + cook time 1 hour
makes 1 pie (serves 6)

MUESLI BARS

2 cups (180g) rolled oats
⅓ cup (50g) sunflower seeds
¼ cup (50g) pepitas)
¾ cup (125g) dried apricots
2 tbsp white chia seeds
2 tbsp boiling water
⅓ cup (25g) shredded coconut
½ cup (125g) butter, chopped
⅓ cup (75g) firmly packed brown
  sugar
2 tbsp honey
½ tsp ground cinnamon

1 Process 1 cup of oats until the consistency of shredded coconut. Add sunflower seeds and pepitas; pulse briefly until a few are coarsely chopped. Transfer mixture to a large bowl. Process apricots, chia seeds, and the boiling water until finely chopped; add to the bowl with coconut.

2 Stir butter, sugar, honey, and cinnamon in a medium saucepan over low heat until sugar dissolves and mixture is smooth; stir into oat mixture until combined, then stir in remaining oats.

3 Remove the basket from the pan of a 5.3-quart air fryer and place on a sheet of parchment paper; trace around the base. Cut out shape ¾ in (2cm) larger than the marked tracing. Grease basket and line with the paper cut-out.

4 Press oat mixture very firmly over the paper; use the base of a glass or an offset spatula to compact the mixture. Insert the basket back into the air fryer pan; at 285°F/140°C, cook for 40 minutes.

5 Remove the basket from the air fryer pan and place on a wire rack to cool completely. Using the paper as an aid, lift the slice from the basket and transfer to a board; cut into 12 bars.

KEEP IT Muesli bars will keep in an airtight container for up to 2 weeks.

prep + cook time 1 hour
makes 12

CONVERSION CHART

MEASURES

One Australian metric measuring cup holds approximately 250ml; one Australian metric tablespoon holds 20ml; one Australian metric teaspoon holds 5ml. North America, New Zealand and the United Kingdom use a 15ml tablespoon.

The difference between one country's measuring cups and another's is within a two- or three-teaspoon variance and will not affect your cooking results. All cup and spoon measurements are level.

The most accurate way of measuring dry ingredients is to weigh them.

When measuring liquids, use a clear glass or plastic bowl with metric markings. We use extra-large eggs with an average weight of 60g each.

DRY MEASURES

metric	imperial
15g	½oz
30g	1oz
60g	2oz
90g	3oz
125g	4oz (¼lb)
155g	5oz
185g	6oz
220g	7oz
250g	8oz (½lb)
280g	9oz
315g	10oz
345g	11oz
375g	12oz (¾lb)
410g	13oz
440g	14oz
470g	15oz
500g	16oz (1lb)
750g	24oz (1½lb)
1kg	32oz (2lb)

LIQUID MEASURES

metric	imperial
30ml	1 fluid oz
60ml	2 fluid oz
100ml	3 fluid oz
125ml	4 fluid oz
150ml	5 fluid oz
190ml	6 fluid oz
250ml	8 fluid oz
300ml	10 fluid oz
500ml	16 fluid oz
600ml	20 fluid oz
1000ml (1 litre)	1¾ pints

LENGTH MEASURES

metric	imperial
3mm	⅛in
6mm	¼in
1cm	½in
2cm	¾in
2.5cm	1in
5cm	2in
6cm	2½in
8cm	3in
10cm	4in
13cm	5in
15cm	6in
18cm	7in
20cm	8in
22cm	9in
25cm	10in
28cm	11in
30cm	12in (1ft)

OVEN TEMPERATURES

The oven temperatures below are for conventional ovens; if you are using a fan-forced oven, reduce the temperature by 20 degrees.

	°C (Celsius)	°F (Fahrenheit)
Very slow	120	250
Slow	150	300
Moderately slow	160	325
Moderate	180	350
Moderately hot	200	400
Hot	220	425
Very hot	240	475

Measurements for cake pans are approximate only. Using same-shaped cake pans of a similar size should not affect the outcome of your baking. We measure the inside top of the cake pan to determine size.

INDEX

ACKNOWLEDGMENTS

DK would like to thank John Friend for proofreading; Hilary Bird for indexing; Renee Wilmeth for consulting on the US edition; and Sophia Young, Joe Revill, Amanda Chebatte, and Georgia Moore for their assistance in making this book. The Australian Women's Weekly Test Kitchen in Sydney has developed, tested, and photographed the recipes in this book.

Project Editor Siobhán O'Connor
US Editor Jennette ElNaggar
DTP and Design Coordinator Heather Blagden
Jacket Designer Maxine Pedliham
Jacket Coordinator Jasmin Lennie
Senior Production Editor Tony Phipps
Senior Production Controller Stephanie McConnell
Editorial Director Cara Armstrong
Art Director Maxine Pedliham
Publishing Director Katie Cowan

DK DELHI
Managing Art Editor Neha Ahuja
DTP Coordinator Pushpak Tyagi
DTP Designers Raman Panwar, Satish Gaur
Pre-production Manager Balwant Singh

First American Edition, 2023
Published in the United States by DK Publishing
1745 Broadway, 20th Floor, New York, NY 10019

A catalog record for this book is available
from the Library of Congress
ISBN 978-0-7440-9009-3

Printed and bound in Slovakia

For the curious
www.dk.com

MIX
Paper | Supporting
responsible forestry
FSC™ C018179

This book was made with Forest
Stewardship Council™ certified
paper – one small step in DK's
commitment to a sustainable future.
**For more information go to
www.dk.com/our-green-pledge**